DIARY
OF A
ZEN
NUN

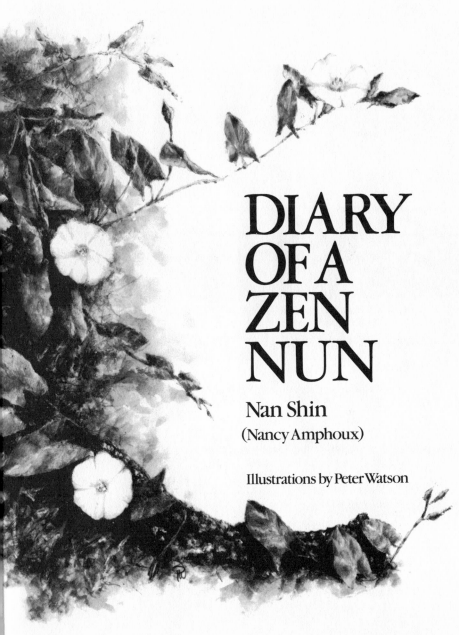

DIARY OF A ZEN NUN

Nan Shin
(Nancy Amphoux)

Illustrations by Peter Watson

E. P. DUTTON | NEW YORK

Published in the United States by
E. P. Dutton, a division of New American Library,
2 Park Avenue, New York, N.Y. 10016.

Library of Congress Cataloging-in-Publication Data

Nan Shin.
Diary of a Zen nun.
1. Nan Shin. 2. Religious life (Zen Buddhism).
3. Zen Buddhists—United States—Biography.
4. Cancer—Patients—United States—Biography.
I. Title.
BQ974.A3587D53   1986   294.3'657   85-27576
ISBN: 0-525-24408-5

Published simultaneously in Canada by
Fitzhenry and Whiteside Limited, Toronto

W

10 9 8 7 6 5 4 3 2 1
First Edition

To Sensei—Taisen Deshimaru Roshi—and Jacob Foguel,
who almost met over breakfast

Deshimaru, Yasuo [Mokudo Taisen], Soto Zen monk, Master, great bodhisattva of modern times. b. Saga City, Kyushu, Japan, November 29, 1914. d. Tokyo, April 30, 1982.

Yokohama Technical College 1933–36. Met Kodo Sawaki Roshi 1936, became lay disciple. Married ca. 1940.

Employed Mitsubishi mining concerns 1940. Sent Borneo 1941 to supervise mining activities (ineligible for military service).

Returned Japan 1946. Various social, religious, economic activities.

Ordained 1965, on eve of master's death. Invited to Europe 1967, settled in France.

Founded Zendonien temple in Loire Valley, over 100 dojos in Europe and elsewhere.

Clubs: none known. Hobby: educating disciples.

Address: ashes divided between temple in Japan, family, temple in France.

Motto: "Continue zazen eternally."

SOME OF THE WORDS USED
BY DESHIMARU ROSHI'S DISCIPLES

THERE ARE ABOUT TWENTY funny-sounding foreign words in this book, which have to do with the activities in a Zen group or center.

Take them as the trappings of the trade and don't worry about them. The drawings may help or may only confuse the issue but in either case they're beautiful.

To run through some of the words most frequently mentioned, just for the hell of it: there is what you do; that is called *zazen*. When you do it you sit on a cushion that is a *zafu* (the artist was afraid his drawing of a zafu looked like a cough drop and it may, but it also looks very much like a zafu).

If you're a monk or a nun you wear certain clothes while doing it (and at other times). First, a white *kimono*, then a black *kolomo*. On top of them goes either a *rakusu*, which is small and hangs round your neck, or a *kesa*, which is large and wraps all around you. Sometimes, you carry another piece of cloth draped over your left forearm—a *zagu*, which you unfold and sit and kneel on during ceremonies.

While you are sitting, you may ask to be smacked on the shoulders with a *kyosaku*, or stick of awakening. If you're literally asleep, you may get smacked without asking. The room in which all this takes place is a *dojo*.

In addition to sitting, there is walking between two sitting periods. That is *kin hin*. Part of the time you're sitting, a big bronze bell sounds outside the dojo (at the temple, but not, of course, in town). That is a *bonsho*. At the end of the sitting in the morning there's a ceremony. During that you chant *sutras*.

If you fidget all the time or if you have to leave early because you're on the kitchen staff or if you come late or if you've got a terrible cough you sit in a corridor running alongside the dojo but outside it, called a *gaetan*. While you're sitting, one person may talk. That is a head teacher, or *godo*. There is another person called a *shuso* who sees that the rules of behavior in the dojo are respected.

As well as sitting and performing ceremonies and eating and sleeping and laughing and staring and talking and so forth, you also work. That is *samu*.

If you do these things for a day or several days or weeks or months, that period is a *sesshin*.

And as long as you practice these things, whether you're ordained or not, you belong to a *sangha,* which is the community of people who practice.

The reason why we use the Japanese (or Sanskrit or whatever) terms instead of finding equivalents in our native languages is not that we have a faddish desire to keep secrets and be mysterious and exotic.

For one thing, they are the words our master used and we continue to use them in memory of him.

But also: why do we say samu instead of work? Because to us they don't mean the same thing. Why do we say zafu instead of cushion? Cushion has connotations that are not shared by the kapok-filled objects on which we sit.

Sometimes, following a common English practice as in the case of musical instruments in an orchestra or positions on a team (second violin, tackle), these words may refer to both persons and things; in fact, they refer to neither, but to functions. Bonsho is the bell but also the person who rings it—really, the ringing; kyosaku is the stick of awakening and also the person who carries it—the awakening, in fact, that includes persons, stick and action.

The experiences are new, and it helps to keep them new if the words are new also. But that's more than enough of them for now, and there are others in the book. As I say, however, never mind them. The time to start worrying is when neither words nor experiences are new any longer. How many times can you breathe this breath?

I had to laugh the other day driving out from Paris in my new car. There I was daring for the first time to open her up, half-terrified at 110 mph and feeling very wicked and exciting, when I suddenly found myself overtaken by myself, the very identical car and color, traveling at 120+ mph. It was so obvious what we both thought we were up to.

So what is this Zen nun who buys Honda Preludes to drive at 110 mph?

And will own nothing but Russian Blue cats and Anglo-Arab horses? And breeds lamprologus brichardi in her fish tanks? And grows English snake's-head fritillary in her garden in the middle of the city of Strasbourg on the Rhine?

Who's kidding who?

white kimono,
black kolomo

THE ALARM, TEN MINUTES before the wake-up bells. Weight of blankets. At the window, a leak of pallor. The bladder urges. Icy floor tiles. Thong sandals, shuffle on. Lurch through chill and dark to door, open, cross hall, open toilet door. The wind must have fallen—the door's not knocking. Back across hall, turn on light, toothbrush and towel, down hall to bathroom behind sewing-room littered with machines and material in every stage of composition, back down hall to room, pour mineral water into glass, twenty drops from one bottle, teaspoonful from another, large dose of vitamin C against the coughs and colds everyone's always catching here—with zazen things come out: old fatigues and old karma; and things go in: cosmic energy and germs (zazen being a very specific form of seated meditation, and karma being action or manifestation, of body, mouth or mind), put on underpants, wool T-shirt, cardigan, white kimono, black kolomo, spectacles on chain, look at list, stuff cigarettes and lighter into kimono sleeve along with sutras, sheet listing services during sesshin, Kleenex. Make bed.

I have
lived almost
fifty years on
this earth, and yes,
after all, there is some-
thing particular.

On this earth . . . the mildest of weary
rhetorical flourishes; but in this case the operative
words.

What made up my mind this morning was the sight of a sort
of small convolvulus with pinkish-white flowers that creeps along
the beige and yellow tractor ruts between the fields where I was
riding. I have seen this little plant or weed every summer day for
years, here in Alsace, and it or a close cousin to it many summer
days in childhood in Illinois, and I have never cared much for it.
Have scarcely seen it hundreds of times, thus, eyes glancing over
it with the faintest flash of disinterest or distaste while scanning for
other plants or insects or beasts or reflections of skies and clouds
in puddles; always discarding it as of no interest, on every occasion,
probably including the first; never bothering to consider what it was
about the plant that caused me to reject it consistently, at the very
threshold of consciousness.

And this morning, noticing as I rode things about the quality
of the heat, the haze, the stage the skylarks had reached in their
summer song, the comparative density of gnats and relative scarcity
of horseflies and casting these various items into an equation involv-
ing the exact week of summer and hour of the morning with an
unspoken view to a comparison between now and how it had all

4

been the day before, month before, year before and how it might all conceivably be tomorrow, my eyes strayed over the little crawling plant and I thought, Even you.

Then, vaguely, I don't know its proper name. It is a pity, really.

Then, with more consciousness and a first flicker of determination, Well, why not after all? How many people can have moled so stubbornly and so unseeing through these fields? If only I could do it like Walton, just walking out of northeast London one morning into a perfection of fish and fishing.

But what shall I use for recipes?

ON THE MATTER OF ILL-
ness: there is a newly formed
cancer group in Strasbourg. At a
meeting recently one woman
who is studying for some advanced degree in psychology
said she would like to tape people talking about their histories
of cancer, it was her idea that the
experience might potentially do

the same work as psychotherapy, would anyone care to volunteer?
I think her idea is correct, at least in some sense or degree, and
volunteered.

Then there is a young Zen monk whose ears prick whenever
I make a reference to those months of chemotherapy, and who said
one day recently under the roar of a well-watered dinner in a
restaurant, "I hear you talk well about death. We must get you to
give us a sesshin before you kick the bucket."

And someone else wrote me, "What I want is to know your
own experience of illness."

Why the interest?

People on their ailments are not always interesting, far from
it. But we all hope for a—must I say the word—recipe, we all
believe, however much we know we shouldn't, that maybe somebody's got that recipe and can show us how not to be sick, suffer
and die.

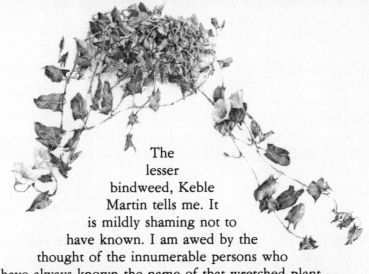

The
lesser
bindweed, Keble
Martin tells me. It
is mildly shaming not to
have known. I am awed by the
thought of the innumerable persons who
have always known the name of that wretched plant.

But one is still not quite content. I would also need to know
its name in French, if I wanted to talk about it in the day-to-day train
of life. And in order to talk about it to the people who see it most
and might conceivably have something to say about it, that it's a
frightful weed and would smother the crops if it got a chance, or
that you can make an infusion of it and cure piles or spots in front
of the eyes, one would need to know what it is called in Alsatian;
and even that would not quite complete the picture because more
than one peasant hereabouts, if he knows its name at all, will know
it in German, and the German name may be totally different from
the Alsatian one.

However: the lesser bindweed. That does something for the
relationship. Would it be right to say it gives one a purchase on the
plant? Does one really "possess" what one can name? I should say
not. Being able to name a thing is, yes, like connecting two dots in
the cosmic outline puzzle. I could say that it often enables me to
dismiss a thing and move on to some other source of anxiety or
uncertainty; but it doesn't seem to me to confer any essential power.
I can't do anything worse to the lesser bindweed now that I know
its name than I could before: if I wanted to tear it up by the roots

I should not need to know what it was called. A slight measure of triumph over the puzzle, thus, is primarily what one gains; and then, because of our being social animals and so forth, the power of exchanging information with others.

But then again. For years, along the roadsides, mainly in France but also Germany and Italy, I have been noticing that stalky, branchy, almost unleaved miniature tree of a weed with the most beautiful blue daisylike flowers in the armpits of its branches. It has been associated with great heat and the rather mournful long drives I tended for years to make between the Mediterranean coast and London or Strasbourg when the holidays were over. For some little time I have wanted to know its name, initially because it seemed so pretty, shapely-stern and fragile without leaves, in amongst the gushing growth of all the other plants. I wanted to know its name because it was pretty.

Then, just recently, I wanted to know its name because I wanted to bring it into my tiny garden and make it grow in that corner that has a curse upon it (or too many thicknesses of dog pee) where nothing seems to survive; and for that purpose it would be necessary to know whether it reproduces by seeds or shoots or what. So in that case, true, one needed to know the name in order to exert power.

I went through Keble Martin the other day in search of the blue plant and didn't find it. But this morning, flushed with encouragement after identifying the lesser bindweed, I became more cunning, or attentive or imaginative, and found it almost at once. The problem was that the drawing didn't look like the plant, but only like one small part of the plant.

Chicory. So simple. And how ironic to learn that it is a "garden escape." There wasn't time at breakfast to investigate further but I can soon know how it grows and whether I want to or can have it in the garden.

I remember a couple of years ago there was some speculative

talk about going to live in North Africa or the Near East. I was intrigued of course but also hesitant. A brief visit to Morocco told me why. The very morning after our arrival I went out to walk in the town and, apart from the orange trees lining the streets, I saw virtually not one tree, bird or plant that I could name. I wrote back home that I would not move to such a country because the task of relearning how everything was called was more than I could face at my age.

But in the first instance, naming seems to me to be an activity engaged in for its own sake.

THE WAKE-UP BELL-RING-ers jog and jangle through the gray, outside on the paths and inside up and down stairs and corridors. Flop down hall to far end and down back stairs to floor below. Remove sandals at door of improvised Buddha hall, bow to statue of Kannon—the spirit of compassion; "who hears the sounds of the world"—remove red-lacquered cups and lids, sandals on, down another half-flight to godo's kitchen. (Godo: the head teacher in a Zen community. The "godo" in these pages are several people. The term is only partly to be confused with an idea of Samuel Beckett's.) Mineral water into teakettle, light gas, plug in coffee machine prepared last night, put salt-pickled plum into teacup ready on tray, empty lacquer cups, put sugar and water in one, stir. Teakettle boils, pour over green Japanese tea in small teapot, stack glasses washed last night on tray ready to go down, pour tea into second red-lacquer cup, take both back up to Buddha hall and place on altar, down to kitchen, look at watch. Fifteen minutes before zazen.

IT WAS SO HOT in Honolulu after Tokyo and we were not dressed for it; also, the people who were supposed to meet us were not there. He was positively bad-tempered because of that, but when they eventually turned up and started throwing leis around the temper disappeared. After lunch we finally got into a hotel and were beginning to wind down a little, when the word came that Sensei wanted to go for a swim. His secretary and I staggered down to the ground-floor shops and bought him a swimming suit—Pierre Cardin. We grabbed something for ourselves, collected him and a taxi, and said, Waikiki.

The taxi dumped us somewhere along the beach and we walked down to the water. It was so good, and hit us like a steam-roller after three weeks of charging around Beijing and Tokyo, temples, chantings, meetings and presentations, uptight, deadly boredom in official offices and smiling to journalists ("Please: what do you Westerners *see* in Zen, so interesting for us.") and squeezing round children and grandchildren in the little apartment of Sensei's wife, and struggling with the Tokyo subway and following Sensei in and out of shops carrying parcels and then all night on the plane.

His secretary and I swam for a while and he sat with our things. When we came out he went down to the water's edge and started playing like a baby porpoise, paddling and splashing in the water and rolling up and down the sand so that it was impossible to tell where he ended and sand and water began.

I looked at him, and his words, "The cosmos and I are one root," went through my head.

This
morning I
was out early
enough, and the sun
was up late enough, for
me to see the lesser bindweed in
its nocturnal guise. The lobes were closed
at the top, taut beneath, swelling at the bottom,
and each lobe was pulling itself in at the edges, clamped to the next,
so that its midrib protruded, giving a suggestion of a star shape to
the closed flower when you looked at it from above; this, combined
with a slight torsion of the whole the cause of which I cannot guess,
made one think of the word *whorl,* and added greatly to what has
already become an attachment. A few minutes later they were all
wide open but I felt that affectionate superiority one does when one
can say, "I know what he/she looks like in bed."

There has been enough rain literally to settle the dust, no
more, and slightly darken the colors of everything. The dust has
been so fine these last days that one saw tracks of partridge and
pheasant and roe deer as though drawn on a page of a book.

There were other things about the morning—but they have
sunk beneath the weight of newscasts, rioting in Poland and
fighting in Chad and Beirut, not to mention all the other places in
the world where there is fighting but it doesn't happen to be in the
headlines today.

I only wonder, and wonder, having never been where fighting
was, or occupations, or famines, or visibly oppressive governments.
I have always lived within sight of trees and, even in Pittsburgh and

London, blackbirds or squirrels or at the least sparrows and am, I suppose, like millions and millions of other people, unable to believe that things can be any other way than I have known them, with crops being planted and harvested and rotated and spring being followed by summer then autumn then winter then spring.

Not only am I unable, at one level, to believe things can be otherwise, I am certain that they need not be. There is nothing inevitable. The actions of the past operate at every instant and so, at every instant, does freedom.

Not without effort, I grant. But can that effort be greater than the effort of conflict?

THE GYNECOLOGIST-SUR-
geon, "user-friendly" if I ever
saw one, chubby and pleased
with his work and himself,
swirled his disc around my belly
and pointed to things on the
screen, took some pictures and
drew circles and outlines on
them and pointed in a brisk but
cheerful manner to one or two
things he didn't like the looks of. I didn't like the looks of any of
it, it looked to me like a cavern with bulbous stalactites and stalag-
mites burgeoning pretty much all over the place. That has to come
out, he said, and if it all has to come out I'm not going to wake you
up to ask your permission. He also said, No, definitely you're not
going on vacation to Israel, what if something there got twisted and
you had to be operated on in emergency conditions.

I said I trusted him and to carry on up the Khyber, and we
shook hands as though we had just completed a highly satisfactory
real-estate transaction.

It was another ten days before rooms and things could be
arranged, during which the ideas of being without my entire repro-
ductive apparatus and of having a cancer somewhere in the lot
knocked round my head but seldom, were discussed at table but
seldom, and lightly, in the matter-of-fact, no-holds-barred style I
seem to have that misleads people about my steadfastness; but these
ideas were neither of them, in any sense, "real." I did have a little
trouble sleeping but that was not unprecedented; the only symptom
of anything amiss was a spate, a positive cataract, of fantasies of
violent death, off the horse's back, at the wheel of the car, and so
forth.

I am afraid of general anesthesia, and said so to the surgeon
beforehand.

He said, You must explain that to the anesthetist who'll be around the night before.

On the night before, various preparations had been made, by which I had not been bothered—the buffer state was already effective—when the door opened and a woman's face appeared in it, nervous, a little hagridden. She gave me a stare and enquired whether I had ever had facial paralysis. I said, Not to my knowledge, and left it at that: an explanation of the generations of twisted smiles in the family seemed something for which this unknown person visibly did not have time. She then announced that she was the anesthetist and I dutifully informed her that I was afraid. Afraid of what, she asked. Of not waking up, I said; of my heart stopping. Oh, the *heart* doesn't give out, she said, and closed the door, having never removed her hand from the knob, leaving me to wonder about all the other things that she seemed to imply *did* give out.

This sort of irritation, of which there was plenty from start to finish, has a very salutary effect on me, bringing out all my aggressiveness and bellicosity. It is a pity that it is not successful with everyone.

TAKE TRAY DOWNSTAIRS, open door, announce, "Your tea is ready," wait for response, go through other door into small sitting room; godo's bell-girl comes up the steps from outside, the boy in charge of ceremony equipment arrives and asks what's needed this morning. The wood sounds outside the dojo—ten minutes.

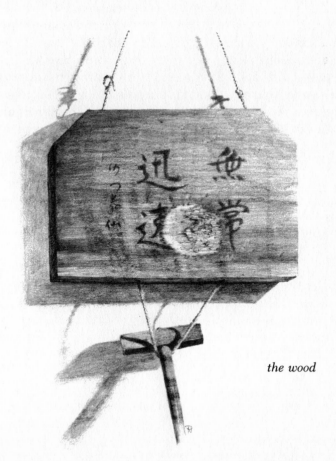

the wood

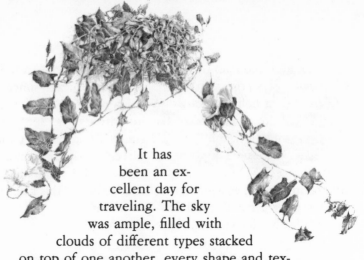

It has
been an ex-
cellent day for
traveling. The sky
was ample, filled with
clouds of different types stacked
on top of one another, every shape and tex-
ture but always, in at least one corner, a spot
or streak of blue. The roads were full of tourists but the verges
seemed cleaner than usual so that the casualties were more noticeable, the flattened hedgehogs, pigeons, cats, small birds identifiable
only by a dab of wingfeathers slanting up out of a smudge on the
surface of the road.

From Mulhouse to Besançon or thereabouts I debated the
nuances of connotation between he/she/they *are* come/gone etc.
or *have* come/gone etc. and why some forms have become obsolete
whereas others are still in use.

I found Argilly without much trouble, but the first person I
asked didn't know the name I was told to ask for and the village
was so quiet, it being lunch time on Saturday, that I decided not to
look further for the friend's house. Off the road to one side was the
spire of the church and I headed for that. The churchyard was
around it, walled—more like an English village than most French
ones. I stopped and sat under a tree and ate and did the weekend
crossword and stared at the houses. None seemed empty, all had
gardens or pots of flowers at the windows. A new house going up
here and there but very few, and almost none in ruins. Stability. I
didn't see a single shop, no baker or post office, and in all two kids

on bikes and one man on foot went past me while I sat. This kind of place always poses questions: is life here better than in the city or is it perfect hell? It seemed so self-contained, there was nothing at all anywhere outside this village. Except, when the wind blew in the right direction, the very faint mumble of the motorway.

After Beaune I drove through the impeccable vineyards of Pommard and Meursault, so regular and level at the tops that they look as though they have been sheared by an electric pruner. At Rochepot two and three years ago there was a horse in a field; automatically I looked and there was a horse but not the same one, I think.

Westward, going through the Morvan, there was Nolay. Who was born there? Or was it Molay. Wait: Molay was something out of my childhood—shaving cream or something of that sort. No; it was Decise where somebody was born, some figure in the French Revolution. Nolay, Molay; and what about Bengay? Or was it Ben-Gay? Or BunGay? BunGay was in Dorothy Sayers, I think—or Wodehouse? Or H. G. Wells? It was Ben-Gay I was remembering. Liniment? The Ben-Gay heiress; was there a Ben-Gay heiress? He's marrying the Ben-Gay heiress, my dear. Was there a family home, was there an old factory somewhere of the sort Simenon transformed into a unique stench of mildew?

East of Bourges come the sunflower fields, I had forgotten. But so stunted, barely two feet tall, and all of them with their ripe heads drooping, facing east. Some of the fields were flattened. Perhaps the result of a combination of a long, very rainy spring, summer drought and recent hailstorms. Or perhaps they were a special variety, deliberately dwarfed for easy harvesting. Uniformly stunted and tormented as they were, and for whatever reason, there they stood, crowded together mile after mile with their heavy heads. Why should this spot on earth be heaven for sunflowers?

Less than an hour from destination I was at last able to leave the thick of the traffic, and since I had plenty of time before dinner

I stopped at a little village hotel-restaurant for a beer and a few blank minutes; but they were almost too blank. There was virtually nobody in the hotel except an uneasy dog, and the beer when I got it was tasteless. I stared at the monstrously deformed face of the woman who eventually produced it, or rather I didn't stare, wondering why she hadn't had it fixed, whether it was fixable, and whether everybody else pretended she wasn't monstrously deformed. She seemed quite cheerful.

And now at the end of the day, this is home.

La Gendronnière, Japanized "Zendonien" by our master. A Soto Zen Buddhist temple in the Loire Valley between Orléans and Tours. A large fake château, lots of outbuildings, the meditation hall and refectory we built ourselves, and, at certain times in the year, some hundreds of us. There are questions and hesitations and uncertainties now that our master has died, and some of us are not here anymore but have gone in search of other masters or quit altogether. But definitely home. In the thirteenth century the founder of the order wrote that the community of monks and nuns —the sangha—were the only real family, the only real friends. As time passes, despite the enormous differences between us all, of background, fortune, lifestyle, education, this becomes increasingly true.

I parked near the three gingko trees planted the first year after Sensei bought the place. Last year they were still encased in their wire cages to protect them, the weeds were taller than they and nobody seemed to be noticing. This year the cages are gone, the trees are taller than the weeds, and the weeds have been pulled. I went up the mound to pay my respects to Sensei's ashes in his tomb. There was no one else around and the deep gravel crunched and sloughed away under my feet. The sound of La Gendronnière: gravel, crunching under the feet of a kyosaku man or woman making the rounds during meditation, under the feet of the lights-out men walking in the night with their wooden clappers, under the feet of late arrivals or early wanderers. You can tell after a while what kind of shoes they're wearing, clogs or sandals or pumps with heels. One becomes very attached to the sound, I find. The audible record of one-foot-in-front-of-the-next, the walker on the Way, our biped species.

This room I have never slept in before. It was a maid's room, on the top floor, with large faded and splotched beef-blood red stone squares on the floor (why did people so weight down the tops of their houses?) and the floor uneven over every inch of its surface. Old paper, beige with pink and green speckles and white squiggles, on the walls, hospital-green woodwork, a damp patch on one wall and another wall in need of a wash, signs of new wiring overlaid on the old and a quick patch job in a wall where some pipe was removed, a good firm low bed, a lamp with nothing to plug it into, a mauve plastic wardrobe, the luxury of a low table, instructions on the wall telling what to do in case of fire, a window looking out the front framing one huge cedar and one huge copper beech. Organize your life for a few weeks quickly, invent an ashtray, a wastepaper basket, find a toilet and somewhere to wash, somewhere to place the official accoutrements of your monk- or nun-hood, unroll your sleeping bag and go to dinner. And after, to the bar in the tent to see the faces you haven't seen, some of them, for a year. Go early to bed because the day will be tiring and this one was too.

No owls; maybe it's only in September that they call so much in the evening. Later in the night you hear them, two kinds, barn and tawny. Sometimes there's a third.

GODO EMERGES FROM HIS bedroom, teacup in hand, storming against the difficulty of turning texts into live teaching and complaining of a sore neck. All three put on kesa. From godo's bedroom, take zagu and papers for oral teaching during zazen. Place set of bowls on table for easy collecting later. From altar in small sitting room take special incense box. The gong rings in the dojo, announcing beginning of zazen. The bell-girl unwraps bell and chings twice. Godo lights a stick of incense at sitting-room altar and comes to the door.

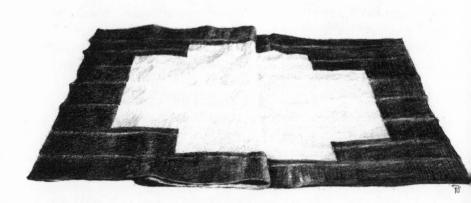

zagu

22

(I OPEN A PARENTHESIS here, for an incident—perhaps the only one—by which I was charmed.

(The next morning, after I had been ladled onto the operating table—why are they always so chilly?—, heard one of the assistants say, as she positioned a leg, "Knee cartilage," and corrected her, "No, patellectomy," with some pride that I was still sufficiently compos to do so, the hagridden lady sat down to her apparatus on my left, made her preparations and suddenly yelled —that is the precise word—in the direction of the anteroom where surgeon and crew were dressing, "Hurry up out there, I'm injecting!"

(What I like to call my sensitivities were offended by this casual treatment, bordering on the boorish, and if I had been in a different position I might have sniffed. It did not, of course, occur to me that the lady was under great pressure herself and if it had I am not sure I could have brought much commiseration to bear just then.

(She had, however, forewarned me so I quickly began reciting to myself the opening syllables of the *Hannya Shingyo* sutra, the central sutra of Soto Zen, KAN JI ZAI BO SAT GYO JIN—and that was that.

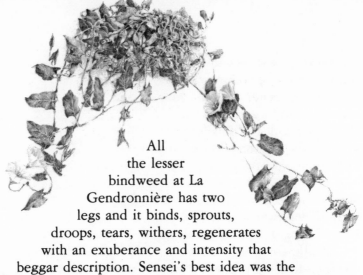

All
the lesser
bindweed at La
Gendronnière has two
legs and it binds, sprouts,
droops, tears, withers, regenerates
with an exuberance and intensity that
beggar description. Sensei's best idea was the
bar, a plastic tent well away from the other buildings, where crêpes
and cakes and pies and soft drinks are sold before and after meals
and before lights-out at night to the hungry, and beer and sake and
hard liquor, on certain evenings, to the otherwise hungry; where
many people go for conviviality without eating or drinking anything, and stare, talk, sometimes dance and on occasion fight. The
floor is pounded dirt, full of dust. You sit on old upholstered
red-plastic benches picked up from some renovated train station.
The place can be dismal with all the dismalness of the parts of
ourselves we dislike and caress, cling to and abhor; the bartenders
can make it gay too, and usually do.

Sensei called it the Bonno Bar (*bonno* meaning illusions, delusions, passions, attachments) and insisted, despite much criticism
and perplexity, some of it well-meaning, that it be allowed to remain; partly because Zen does not exclude anything and tolerance
is good for us all—especially, perhaps, the saintly; partly because it
is a source of income and not to be sneezed at on that account;
partly because it is better for us to wash our dirty linen among
ourselves than to descend upon an innocent countryside and gain
an unsavory reputation for ourselves; and partly because we bring

our illusions with us and are seldom if ever separate from them so it is inaccurate, if nothing more, to pretend one is "retreating" into spirituality. Better that illusions should be seen and heard, he thought, and forgotten. Leave fewer traces, create less karma. But do not try to leave none at all or create no karma.

Hence, the bar. Do not believe what you may hear about abstemious vegetarian Zens; although they may be in the majority.

On party nights, at two or three or four in the morning the lesser bindweed whirls round a superb bonfire the heart of which would cook your Joan of Arc in the twinkling of an eye, under a breathtaking velvet sky strewn with particular stars.

And these people are profoundly religious. Some of them are also a mess. But if you pick fifteen hundred or two thousand people anywhere, some of them are going to be a mess.

THE MINIBUS TOOLED AROUND the hillsides above
Honolulu and we were all groggy with exoticism, new birds, plants
undreamed of, island atmosphere; so when the bus pulled up at the
entrance to some sort of park I was unprepared. The Pearl Harbor
memorial cemetery it was; and why on earth the Soto Zen bishop
of Hawaii had included it on the itinerary I cannot imagine.

We piled out, and I, who somehow hadn't realized that Pearl
Harbor was *here* (my grandfather was temperamental and flew
readily off the handle, I had witnessed many emotions coming from
him but they all passed lightly, quickly; so that day, when he sat for
hours in his armchair in the corner of the living room huddled next
to the radio cabinet, listening so intently that his eyes were looking
nowhere, and from him rolled waves of weariness, attention, reor-
ganization—how is it going to be for us, what will we have to
do—, as the bombing of Pearl Harbor was announced and war
declared, I crouched there, not too close because all the ominous
significance in that corner of the room scared me badly, and
watched him, and had no idea, no idea at all), hung behind the rest
to catch my breath a little and try to take in this place.

Sensei and the bishop trotted over to the monument and began
chanting a *Hannya Shingyo,* followed by the rest of the group.
Staring at those two small Japanese men, who suddenly seemed so

self-assured, even smug, chanting away at their Zen Buddhist sutra in front of a memorial to my countrymen who died because their countrymen wanted a war (I couldn't know that my countrymen wanted it too), my mind reeled, suddenly they were the enemy again, suddenly I hated black robes again, hated Oriental mumbo-jumbo again, hated religions again and their fire-breathing and propitiating and pretense of going beyond enmity and overcoming egotisms; in short, suddenly I was five years old again.

So I went to sit under a tree and change the film in my camera while they chanted. I joined them as they got back into the minibus and Sensei turned to me and said, very plainly and not scolding, "When I sing you must sing." I said, "Yes, Sensei."

That afternoon on the flight to Los Angeles I explained, partly —not about hating them as jolly little Japanese who always had an answer for everything, but about how I hated monuments and memorials erected by grateful governments because, I said, governments are never grateful, people maybe but not governments, and memorials are not for the dead but for the living, to control them and keep them ready to make more wars and have monuments erected to themselves. He stared at me. He didn't understand; because, I suppose, for him government was government and had nothing to do with what he was doing when he was chanting a reconciliatory sutra in front of the memorial at Pearl Harbor. He didn't understand, but he was always attentive to the things that really bothered people.

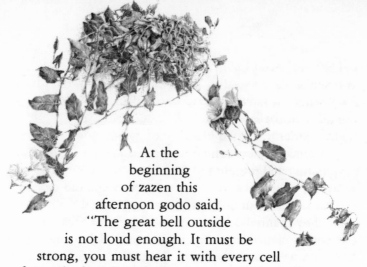

At the
beginning
of zazen this
afternoon godo said,
"The great bell outside
is not loud enough. It must be
strong, you must hear it with every cell
of your body." Somebody went to tell the bell-
ringer to put more muscle into it.

I thought, with a sour little occupational reflex, trite, "every cell of your body." He means, Listen hard.

Then: the simple truth, of course, is that every cell of your body does hear it. Or does it, if you don't know it does?

If you don't know it does then some cells at least are not hearing, maybe they all aren't. Because consciousness, knowing, involves cells.

From that I concluded, wearily, that to say our language is approximate or vague or whatever is a mistake. What our language is, very often at any rate, is devastatingly accurate.

It must be our minds that are sloppy. And yet our minds are at least partly the creators of that devastatingly accurate language, than which only silence is more accurate still.

One thing certain is that we do not pay enough attention enough of the time.

(THE NEXT DAY WHEN I was out of the vapors I asked Jean, who had sat with me some time the day before while I was still full of tubes, whether I had said anything interesting. He said, No, you said nothing at all, except of course to moan now and then, and then one word, "Fizz," several times, drawing it  out with some delectation. Fizz! Then I remembered that I had gone out when I reached JIN in the *Hannya Shingyo,* and laughed at the shift in my unconscious or whatever that had slipped out of the recital of the highest wisdom and basis of Zen metaphysics and into a connection dating from the years of early adolescence when I was learning how to drink in Illinois. Gin fizz indeed. So much for the loftiness or profundity of one's unconscious murmurings in extreme situations.)

There followed some unhappy days. I made the acquaintance of hallucinations, which I suppose had to do with anesthesia and chemicals charging around my system; and the room I was in stuck out of the façade of the moderately decrepit suburban clinic and had windows on three sides of it so that the wind, which was quite high at the end of March, rattled and shrieked around me night and day and I was extremely cold. It was also not far from the maternity ward, or rather from the place where babies were kept when not with their mothers, and one poor little blighter seemed to be badly upset and screamed for a great part of the night, several nights running. I ached a lot more for that baby than in my own body, which did not cause any great pain but disconcerted me when I shifted from side to side because of all that extra room inside it. Things slid about and flopped, rather.

I was further disconcerted a few days later after discovering a scale in one of the nurses' rooms and standing on it: I had shed seven kilos, over fifteen pounds. The gynecologist-surgeon tossed that off with, Why, what I took out of you weighed half that much. But he was very evasive about results and how long I'd have to stay there. Don't rush them in the lab, he said, the more time they have the more sections they'll cut and the less chance there is of them overlooking something.

Tension was, of course, mounting but again I was more aware of momentary unpleasantnesses—getting one's "intestinal transit" going again, now there's a real anguish and a real pain—than of the mounting tension. I asked Jean to try to find out something from him—man-to-man, I thought, he might speak out more. But no.

First
morning of
sesshin. 6 A.M.
The wake-up bells in
the runners' hands jangle
roughly and loud, never exactly in
time with their strides as they trot around
the outsides of tents and buildings and pound up
and down stairs and along corridors inside the main building. The
great copper beech, taller than the highest chimney pot and leaved
solid to the grass, black in the predawn mist, is enormous, awesome.
An owl, close and intimate in the night, calls far off and drowsy in
the woods. People hurry quietly across the gravel and along the
paths. The wood sounds for zazen.

At 10:30 A.M. the beech stands severe, dull and intent in a still,
sunless, windless morning. The wood sounds.

At 4:30 P.M. the beech spreads, splendid, its prime of life,
inhabited by millions, under a late summer sky cleared at last of
mist. The wood sounds.

At 8:30 P.M. the beech muses in gathering twilight, its overpowering presence muted by the countless events of the day. The
wood sounds.

10:30 P.M. Away to the right, in a starless, moonless night, a
point of light glows faintly on the altar of Sensei's tomb. A screech
owl. The lights-out men walk slow and steadily over the gravel,
along the paths, around the tents and buildings, rhythmically clapping their wooden blocks. The beech is invisible.

zafu

THE BELL-GIRL LEADS THE way into the damp, chilly dawn, striking the handbell from time to time. Sandals scrunch across the gravel. The bonsho ringer stands by the great bronze bell, looking exposed but in fact padded in numerous layers under his kolomo and kesa. Godo ignores him and crunches on. Through the dojo window, rows of heads and backs. Kick off sandals and twitch them neatly to one side. Walk

dojo

between 220 pairs of assorted footwear, all pretty carefully arranged, and through door to gaetan, filled this morning with kitchen staff, where it is a little warmer. Bow at entrance to dojo, place papers on reading stand in front of godo's high chair to right of entrance, move to center, unfold godo's zagu, back up, unfold own zagu, perform three prosternations; pick up own zagu, pick up godo's zagu, march round hall behind 220 backs, while godo tours hall and gaetan. Plump up godo's zafu, plump up own zafu, bow to it, turn, bow to backs of everybody else, sit, arrange legs, kolomo, kesa, hands, neck, head.

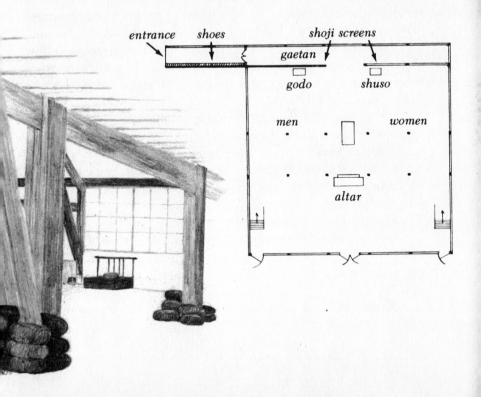

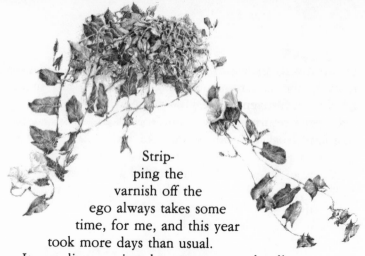

Strip-
ping the
varnish off the
ego always takes some
time, for me, and this year
took more days than usual.
It was discouraging, because one can hardly
avoid entertaining the illusion that asininity should
decrease with assiduous practice.

The first day back on the horse was still a hot dry day, but in those two weeks the season had slipped and shifted, the sky more powdery and pale, the light beginning to slant more. All the summer crops have been harvested, so that now the sheets of yellow grain have vanished and most of the surface is stubble or bare, leaving only the more complicated autumn crops: corn, tobacco, sugar beets and cabbages.

Cabbages. One long gentle slope of hill is all planted in cabbages, and riding along the bottom of it I looked up and there was nothing in the world except these dusky silver-blue knobs, greenish where the sun shone through a single leaf with its thick veins and curl, and an empty pale-blue sky, neither matching nor jarring, only sharply different.

Golden Gate is unmoved by colors.

The wagtails have also gone. I flushed once three and another time four partridge, and remembered that very soon the guns would begin to pop and we should have to be careful. If it isn't the bloody insects it's the bloody guns.

Silence has also begun, relatively, to fall. Passing by one unmown hayfield I was aware of a racket, a positive din, emanating from it. Insects. I remembered years ago being at Consolation in the Jura in November and walking one evening through such a field, then returning to the same field the next morning after the first hard frost: the silence was appalling.

THERE HAD BEEN SEVERAL busy, strange days in New York, trips to the top of the World Trade Center, parties in Greenwich Village where the tables were littered with marijuana cigarettes and he realized it shortly after walking through the door, and also realized that he was being displayed by the hosts but decided to stay anyway: he loved to watch people dancing and he needed to see as much "West" as he could; séances in a beauty parlor in New Jersey, prowls through Chinatown in search of herbs and simples in dim, tight-jawed shops; rides through Central Park and boat trips around Manhattan, with Sensei posing like any other Jap to have fifty-three pictures taken of him with the Statue of Liberty in the background.

Then this short flight to Montreal. I knew he didn't feel much more comfortable in airplanes than I did and I was beginning to learn that he would not turn up until the minute before takeoff, perhaps because he didn't want to spend any more time than necessary inside the infernal contraption and certainly because he wanted to tease me who, as trip organizer, was roaring in anguish at the thought of missed flights, telephone calls, added cost; before the end, I learned my lesson.

The plane landed in Montreal and we all got up and waited to be let off. He sat on the arm of an aisle seat and bounced a leg up and down. It was a sharp, bright autumn morning. He was going to meet a new group, give interviews, appear on television, generally stir things around. I looked down and asked, "Content, Sensei?" He glanced up and said, "Pass. Pass." Which was his shorthand for, "Get rid of that. On to the next." I wondered.

IT MUST HAVE BEEN A good ten, maybe twelve days after the operation when the gynecologist-surgeon tripped in and stood at the foot of the bed and Yes, it was positive, he said. Not then, or ever, did he say where or how much. You'll have to do a course of chemotherapy, he said, over at the cancer clinic. You'll go see the head chemotherapist there, I'll give you a letter and don't let yourself be fobbed off on anybody else, he's the husband of the anesthetist I work with (gasp!) and I said to her at the time of the operation that I thought this would be something for her husband (bloody presumptuous of you). You'll make an appointment for the end of April. Then after the chemotherapy we do another operation to see whether it's worked or not.

Slowly, slowly, I said, You know I'm into Zen and things and alternative and parallel medicine and all that and I don't know whether I agree to this chemotherapy or not.

Suddenly he stopped being Twinkletoes and turned into the Big Bad Ogre, and the end of his peroration was, You're not going to do a Steve McQueen on me. And then he left.

An old Hollywood script might indicate "Begins to weep" at that point, and on ninety-nine occasions out of a hundred I do not follow old Hollywood scripts although they are what I was brought up on but in this instance, lo and behold, no sooner was the door closed than I began to weep.

Jean came in a very few minutes later and sat on the bed and hugged me a bit and called me by a name he never used. Alarm bells instantly went off: I was pretty certain it was a name he had for his wife, who had died of cancer. And I realized that I wasn't going to be able to turn myself over to him in a lump because he was going to be having plenty of trouble himself dealing with this second cancer in his second woman, and he does not talk about his troubles, to anybody. Two women, two cancer deaths—too much, poor taste, grotesque!

That brought me back into a sort of focus.

It was a matter of where do I start, what do I do?

ONE GONG—GODO BOWS to zafu. Second gong—godo bows to everybody. Third gong —godo hoists himself into high chair. A soft, deep bong outside: the great bell, beginning its ringing away of illusions that will continue at roughly two-minute intervals throughout the first period of meditation.

On the left, the notetaker, pen, paper and tape recorder. On the right, legs of godo's chair, him wriggling his legs and clothes into place above—pause while he bows to shuso, who in our group is the person responsible for the dojo itself and the visible behavior of everyone in it, presenting kyosaku—more wriggling.

Above, in the opening between the screens, the heads of two kyosakus, man and woman, pass on their way out to make the rounds, see who's asleep, who's sick. Their shoes crunch away over the gravel in opposite directions. In front, the wall. Silence.

Some minutes later godo leans over: "Have you got a sutra book on you?" "No." "Get one."

Stand up, slip out behind wood-strip curtain. Sandals on, edge across gravel—it's possible to do it without making noise but you have to go slowly—to main building, up steps, into godo's room, get sutra book, out again, a look to the east: behind the clump of oaks and the mound in the middle with the tombstone at the end there are clouds but the sun may rise over them, slowly back to the dojo, through the curtain and into place again.

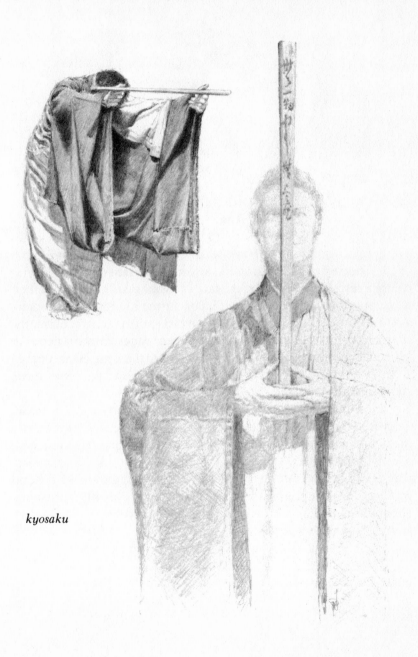

kyosaku

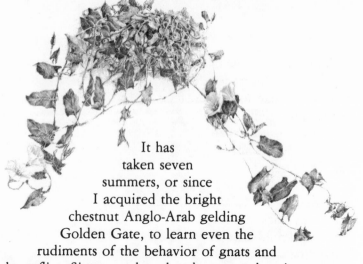

It has
taken seven
summers, or since
I acquired the bright
chestnut Anglo-Arab gelding
Golden Gate, to learn even the
rudiments of the behavior of gnats and
horseflies. Since one has already accepted various
compromises through the mere fact of owning an animal, whether
it be for pleasure or utility, one is condemned before one starts to
a sort of rubbing-along situation in which priorities are constantly
shifting with circumstances and the keen edge of one's need to
learn is very much dulled. It has therefore taken me all this time.

Without the horse, on the other hand, I should never have
come even this far.

Horseflies, or gadflies as they are also called, are the worst.
They fasten on to your animal and chomp away, leaving raw bleed-
ing spots and raising great weals. Being so singleminded and
greedy, however, they are very easy to swat, using a flat noisy slap
that does not frighten the horse. Gnats, or midges, are no serious
problem to you unless by some freak one should fly into both eyes
at once, but you must learn to respect them as a true ordeal to the
animal; it would seem that they get lost inside those furry large ears
and the whine of them drives the horse very nearly berserk.

There is an arsenal of sorts that one can use against them. The
horse can be sprayed or daubed with a liquid before you go out:
the insects don't like the smell of it and stay away. This lasts exactly
as long as the horse is dry; once he begins to sweat his own smell

predominates and the flies home in on him again. If the day is not so hot that the horse is sweating before you start, you can walk as far as you mean to go and then come back at a gallop, but that creates other difficulties.

Heading stablewards, for instance, the horse may pull your arms out of their sockets or run clean away and into some tractor; and if he doesn't and you get him home it will take you an hour to walk him dry, unless it's so hot he never dries.

There is, of course, the switch or crop. Mine waves rapidly and incessantly back and forth between my head and the horse's; it is effective in mild encounters but no use at all when confronted by a mass attack. One can break off a branch but one seldom picks the right branch; they bend and fold up or aren't long enough and I like to leave branches on trees where possible. There are commercial fly whisks for snobs or fastidious professionals. There are crocheted ear-coverings with tassels like old farm horses used to wear; these, if you don't mind looking silly, are effective against gnats but irrelevant to gadflies.

There is the time of day: if you can get out before the sun gains real heat you will be left relatively in peace. That can mean riding at 5 or 6 A.M. I do not recommend the late evening; it is still hot then and what you gain in gadflies, so to speak, you lose in mosquitoes.

There is also a laterality about all this: these insects tend to fly on the shady side, so if you have a shady side you can concentrate your waving and slapping there, leaving you one arm free to deal with the reins—and you may need it: the horse's tail will take care of his hindquarters, more or less, but occasionally a fly attaches itself to his belly beyond the reach of his tail and he will then stop, even at a gallop, and attempt to kick it off with one hind hoof, leaving you on your fanny in a field unless you have a strong and quick grip with your legs and at least one hand.

There is, most favorable of all weapons, a breeze. Gnats are not strong fliers and only come out in force on still days. Gadflies are proof against a light breeze, although it seems to inhibit them somewhat, but anything approaching a wind will leave you almost unassailed and with luck able to turn your mind to other considerations momentarily. For do not be deceived: on a good day for gnats and gadflies your ride will consist of nothing else.

There is, as an absolute last resort, speed. Speed has definite disadvantages in hot weather, however, as previously explained, and if you want to have a horse at all to tease the flies with tomorrow you had best use it sparingly. A short gallop will occasionally leave them behind, because they seem to be relatively territorial and do not like to venture many hundreds of yards from their base; but if they are very hungry or angry they will follow some way, especially when hunting in packs, and you will then have no choice but to swat, slap, scream and kick and be bitten, swearing never again. A good trot will keep the bulk of them hovering alongside but not landing and those that do get a hold on the sides of the horse's neck or flanks can be struck down. Flies on the face are primarily the horse's concern, but not only: you do not see them but he feels them and will often stop short, as with a fly on the belly, to rub them off with a foreleg.

The woods are to be eschewed, as harboring more of them than the open fields. Opinion is divided on this point, however, and indeed my own experience is that it all depends. On the whole, I avoid woods, cattle, vineyards, standing water, tall hedgerows and low places; which doesn't leave much.

It is a commonplace that they are worse before storms, and of course it is true; I don't know why. Horses are also "worse" before storms, and at such times there may come one of those moments of total unison they are always writing about in books, when the animal is driven to the extreme limit of its tolerance and breaks for home, whatever curbs or goads you may possess to threaten it with; and you suddenly concur utterly in its decision and are limp with gratitude to the beast for showing so much sense and sparing you yet another display of stoicism.

This morning there occurred a rare combination of luck and cunning. I was late out and that was bad; but there was a palpable breeze so I thought one might take the chance. Riding across the breeze proved useless, the flies all congregated on the leeward side and began their dreary grinding meal. In a flash I realized that the breeze was from the east and the sun still more east than south; so we cantered away to the west and came back at a walk along the highest track, to get the full benefit of movement in the air. There was a brief half-hour of near-victory, the horse walking into the breeze with almost no shadow on either side of him. I had time to notice that the lesser bindweed is not pinkish white as I said before (the book said pink and white); some of the flowers are pink and white, some are white, none are pink. I shall soon find them pretty.

I also had time to have my memory jogged by the precept about not killing. Indeed, I only want the flies not to bite the horse, I don't positively want them dead, and perhaps some recover from one's swats and live to bite again.

Most of the time, that is, I don't positively want them dead. But the other day, coming home late with a friend along the edge of the woods on very hot and weary horses, we were taken unawares by several thousand gadflies in serried ranks. Abandoning everything, we rose in our stirrups and let the horses go at as much of a headlong gallop as they could muster, our arms flailing away at their sides. My crop flew into the air and will never be seen again. The friend behind called out that I was squashing at least two of them with my buttocks at every stride. We burst into hysterical laughter at the sight of ourselves and during those few minutes, flying over the stubble and between the fields of corn with all the elegance of Ichabod Crane, I became an organism possessed by a lust to murder every horsefly in the universe.

GODO IS SPEAKING ABOUT the bar—it had been instructed to quit serving exactly when the lights-out people came through with their clappers and that worked for a couple of nights, but the more enthusiastic drinkers learned how to order three or four drinks at the last moment, which could keep them going for some time, and last night one force of nature bullied the barman into serving after hours so that more people than usual went to bed late and groggy.

Godo orders: *"Rensaku* for the barman and his two assistants." (Rensaku means a varying number of not very painful blows on the trapezius muscles on each side of the back.)

A series of smart thwacks, seven on each side, on the men's half of the dojo—a pause—again on the women's half—a longer pause —then out on the gaetan.

Is this punishment?

Not quite. It is taking note of a breaking of the rules, and finishing it.

Guilt and remorse have no place here. The past is over. Only the right action, now, counts; right for the whole group. And as circumstances are never the same twice, this minute's right action will not be right tomorrow. This is a community, so there are rules; but no rule.

Silence.

I CAME OUT OF HOSPITAL and rang Sensei. I knew he was very ill. He wasn't in Paris but at La Gendronnière, resting for a few days before going back to Japan for treatment. Yes; he said I could come.

Three days later I was on the train. It was a sunny afternoon in the Loire Valley, but cool. Sensei was outside sitting in the sun listening to a Japanese tape, mournful woman's singing. He looked at me and asked how long ago the operation had been; seventeen days, I told him. For you, right, he said. He himself had refused surgery in Europe.

I also told him that I now knew where the *hara* was. Of course one had known before (it's the center of energy and activity, a little beneath the navel; by extension, the abdominal region); but when, two days after the operation, I wanted to stretch out a hand to pick something up and couldn't because all the machinery below the navel was disconnected, I understood in a far more concrete manner that all movement, even of the fingertips, has its origin there.

When one of the girls came back from work and shopping that evening she brought a book by Michio Kushi in French, *Cancer et Alimentation,** which she had found in a shop in Blois. I had thought about a macrobiotic diet but had an idea that if I was going to have highly toxic chemotherapy a sort of light, delicate, sensitive diet would be the wrong thing. After reading the book that night I changed my mind.

The next day I picked up another book on the shelves in Sensei's secretary's room, about treatment by fasting. It didn't ap-

Macrobiotic Approaches to Cancer (Cancer Control Society, 1981).

peal so much, maybe because it was too much one man's argument whereas the Kushi book was full of case studies.

The following day I left. Sensei said, Be careful what you eat. (I translated: go macrobiotic. He had spent a lot of time unclenching the teeth of the hard-core "macrobes" who were among his first supporters when he arrived in Paris and getting it clear in people's heads that Zen and macrobiotics had nothing or almost nothing to do with each other and the title of Ohsawa's book, *Le Zen Macrobiotique,* was an unfortunate mistake; but he also said on many occasions that macrobiotic eating was right for sick people.) He also said, Take medicine. (I translated: have your chemotherapy, mix your own cocktail.)

How
one thing
leads to another.
I must remember one
day to write about how one
thing does not lead to another.
But in this case, it does: this morning,
riding along the canal on the way to the bridge, I
noticed another sort of convolvulus, larger and all white and with
fewer flowers. Of course it has always been there (off and on) but
one hadn't registered before. This, I must presume until I can check
with Keble Martin, will be a greater bindweed. One has, so to
speak, connected two new dots in the universe for the price of one.

You will have observed a certain hesitancy in these writings,
a lot of "almost," "relatively," "nearly" and so forth. Why this
diffidence?

The reason is that I have yet to work out in my bumbling
empirical fashion a single hypothesis about the behavior of things
and organisms without seeing it contradicted almost (but not always) at once. One's hypotheses grow more and more refined and
qualified and in the end one is responding on a purely ad hoc basis,
as, here and now a nightingale is singing and in this place there was
no nightingale last year, full stop; or, this clump of asters is more
advanced than that clump five yards away and it may have to do
with the amount of direct sunlight, but it may have to do with soil
moisture or fertilizer or something else or none of the above.

This morning's instance is: I recall writing only a short time
ago that gnats were "not strong fliers." Well, you can forget that

for a start. This morning there was a positive breeze—from the west, granted, and tepid, but a distinct, strong although erratic, breeze, some people would have spoken of a "wind"—, a hint of rain but as yet no rain. The horse and I sallied forth cheerfully, feeling that a gadfly or two more on one's conscience would be but a small price to pay for a look at the countryside and a smell of the new-mown second crop of hay and a leisurely canter to loosen up the old joints.

Well; the gnats were there too in their myriads, winging bravely alongside and making straight for the equine ears.

Another instance: it is August 1, and the "rule" or general principle is that the orioles, being early leavers, are gone by now. I cocked an ear this morning and heard nothing but the welcome rustle of poplar and corn in the aforementioned strong breeze. For a solid hour, passing near oriole haunts, nary a sound. I was tentatively about to confirm the general principle and announce to the world that the orioles had gone when, just as I was unsaddling, one *twirlyooed* out its mellow call. Saved from making a fool of myself yet again. Thank you, oriole.

This goes to show how pathetically eager we are to get it all shaped up in boxes and files, and why, or at least one reason why, the masters reject generalizations and rules and tell you that silence is best. You may think for a long time that they are trying to be cute or mysterious or unscientific. I begin to suspect they are simply being accurate.

EDUCATING, AS SENSEI CALLED it, took precedence over everything else—sometimes to the detriment of his public image, about which he cared a good deal in the ordinary way.

In Marrakech the first afternoon, we were wandering around the great square, Djemaa El Fna, and as it was February and not many tourists the beggars had little material to work on. We teased and chatted with girls wanting coins "for earrings" ("If I had another it would make a pair.") and shoeshine men, and at one point there was quite a crowd around us. One boy, ten or so, thrust a stump of an arm in Sensei's face. I don't know whether he knew that children are sometimes maimed on purpose; but he was much opposed to begging, Buddhist tradition notwithstanding, and believed that for the sake of the cosmic order people should carry their own weight.

He stared for a fraction of a second, then violently dashed the arm away and strode off. I don't know whether that made any impression on the boy or other onlookers but it did on me, once I got over my initial, social gasp.

Then, in Montreal, there was a press conference one afternoon, several journalists and photographers and thirty or forty other people. One man came accompanying a tiny shrunken woman—a boatperson who had been saved and nursed more or less back to life in Canada and who had expressed a desire to see a live Buddhist master.

There was a clear expectation of saintliness in the air that afternoon, and toward the end Sensei, exasperated by it and wanting to smoke, lit a cigarette. Shock, shock. He said, "Must not be narrow." True spirituality is not in social conventions.

People prepared to go, and the boatperson and her watchdog came forward. It was explained to Sensei that she was a person who had suffered greatly and had come specially to see the Zen master. He looked her hard in the face for an instant, stood up and brushed past her and out of the room.

He risked loss of image when he did things like that; but he cared more about educating.

Which is more useful to a person, pity and compliance (he did comply with his dug before he suck'd it) and nostalgia over the past, or a jolt that makes you see straight where you are now?

It depends. Sometimes, most certainly, the latter.

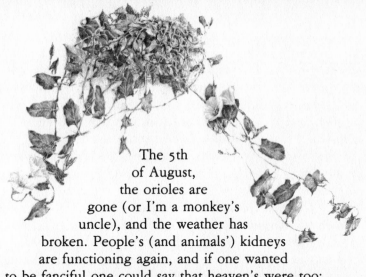

The 5th
of August,
the orioles are
gone (or I'm a monkey's
uncle), and the weather has
broken. People's (and animals') kidneys
are functioning again, and if one wanted
to be fanciful one could say that heaven's were too:
it has rained. The temperature has fallen from ninety-four or ninety-
five degrees to about sixty-five.

So this morning was well-nigh perfect for riding. No bugs at
all. What happens to the gadflies when it cools off; are they brood-
ing lethargically under leaves, or do they die and it's a new generation that rises with the temperature next week or next year or
whenever?

The sky is covered with low solid cloud but it is not grim or
threatening: soft, soft-edged, with faint variations of gray, pearl,
peach, bluish. Quiet cloud. Everything else has become quiet, too.
No larks rose this morning; the only birds I heard were an invisible
horde in trees near the stable; does that mean they are already
beginning to mass for departure? And then one buzzard, mewing
out of sight somewhere.

We rode up to the top of the hill from which we can see the
village where Golden Gate used to live. He always stops there to
stare but I never know if it is recognition, a question in his brain,
or wistfulness to be back in his adolescence when spavin and em-
physema were not present concerns and a kick in the air was a kick
in the air instead of what it has now become, an effortful defiance

of discomfort and a working life. I have found a homeopathic vet for him and he is swallowing sugar lumps soaked in arnica and *rhus tox.* every day with, it seems to me, some results: he is more deliberate about the hindquarters and also more careless, his head dips less at a walk when he has to pull at a stiffening hock.

In the woods there were strange plants (I must have seen them before but cannot remember them), low leafless pillars with bunches of bright orange berries at the top. A very meaningful-looking plant, as if it had been worshiped or feared for millennia. (It turns out to be the fruit of cuckoopint.)

A quiet day. At the top of the hill, looking out over miles of farmland and village and woods, hardly a sound. The corn has tasseled and was rustling faintly, faintly, making even less noise than the pylons, when one drew near them, their wires crackling and throbbing softly with ominous, urgent, indecipherable communication.

An intimate sort of a day, when the thoughts in one's head seem louder, more distinct, when it is easier to string them together and forget how little they weigh in the general scheme of things.

A WOMAN WHO WAS AT La Gendronnière those same days gave me the address of another woman who had had ovarian cancer and gone macrobe and was still cheering the home team at seventy-odd. Back in Strasbourg, I wrote to her. She gave me the name of a top homeopathic doctor in Paris. I made an appointment, but ultimately didn't keep it.

Another friend in Strasbourg came by to visit a couple of days after my return, bringing a book she had picked up in, I think, a supermarket, the title of which, translated, is something like *What They Don't Tell You About Cancer.* I plunged into that. It was highly technical, a survey of all the way-out and not-so-way-out forms of diagnosis and treatment *not* recognized, to put it mildly, by the feudal French medical establishment. Written by a doctor, published in Switzerland. I rang the publisher and they gave me the doctor's address and phone number in the south of France. I rang and made an appointment for the end of the month, just before I was supposed to begin the chemotherapy.

I bumped into other names, in connection with macrobiotics. One a man whose wife had written the first pleasing and unaustere macrobiotic cookbook. I found out where he lived, telephoned, learned he was in Paris at a big alternative-products fair, went there. From him I got the name of a doctor right in Blois, oddly enough (La Gendronnière is nine miles from Blois), who specializes in Oriental diagnosis, iridology and diet. I rang him and made an appointment for the day after the one in the south of France.

I started cooking for myself, being on extended sick leave and not having to go to the office, and I started looking for a cook who would bring meals to me in the weeks I would spend at the cancer clinic if I had the chemotherapy. I found one almost at once, a musician who happened to be out of work at the time and needed a reason to get out of bed before midafternoon.

I made an appointment with a highly reputed homeopathic doctor, who specializes in the anthroposophical treatment of cancer, using injections of an extract of mistletoe. A fair number of my friends are into anthroposophy and although it has never been very congenial to me I thought I'd see. That was a mistake: I had to sit four hours in the waiting room, which is apparently par for the course, and when I did see him he heard me say what had been removed surgically and where, and promptly replied that the first thing to do was to ascertain the location and size of the tumor. I concluded that he was overworked and overtired and not, for me at least, reliable.

I had heard there was a sophrologist in town and he happened to be a doctor I'd had round once for an ear infection. I made an appointment with him. That would have been useful if I had not been a Zen nun and knew what he was saying already, but it did no harm to hear it again. Be here and now, in short.

AT THE END OF ABOUT forty-five minutes, the inside gong: two strokes. Kin hin (an extremely slow walk between periods of seated meditation). Much coughing and clearing of throats. Everybody rises, more or less creakily, plumps up zafus and stacks them against walls and pillars, straightens clothes, shakes numb feet, turns to join one of ten rectangles and begins the almost motionless walk that remains an enigma for many people for years (apart from its obvious use in decongealing bones and blood between two sits). After another few minutes, one gong stroke and all walk quickly back to their sitting places.

There are no platforms and assigned places, and almost no hierarchy of "high" seats. Sensei said to stay in one place throughout, as much as possible, and told more senior disciples to sit near him and those wearing kesas to sit in the back row; but then he divided the men and women so only the men were able to sit near him, and even before he died there was a tendency for the more irregular, headstrong or hungover elements, senior or not, to congregate at the back of the hall where they could look out the French windows and be partly hidden from a godo's view by the altar.

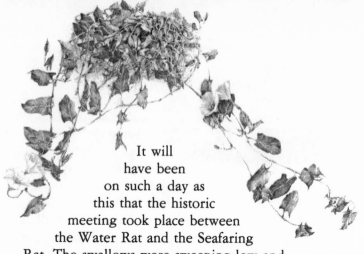

It will
have been
on such a day as
this that the historic
meeting took place between
the Water Rat and the Seafaring
Rat. The swallows were sweeping low and
hurriedly, although they didn't seem really ready
to go. The clouds were marching steadily, and the sky between them
had become a much deeper blue, the kind that pulls you toward it.
The wind was rough and dry, although there will no doubt be storms
in its wake. Golden Gate and I had the first real run we have had for
well over a year, I should think. We went down to the long meadows
between the flour mill and the motorway and there, off the path to
the side, the earth was not too hard for a gallop. On the run back, as
always, he began pulling like a train and it took four huge circles,
each time over a couple of acres, to get hold of his head—although
even then he wasn't running flat out. I think only racehorses in the
straight can run flat out; even polo ponies and cow ponies couldn't
keep upright if they were going at top speed on a curve. Also, I
hadn't shortened the stirrups and was by no means urging him on,
being always afraid of mole holes and wire fences rising up out of
nowhere. But there were still tears streaming down my face from the
wind. And he stopped puffing almost at once and dried quickly, and
there was nobody out with a gun, and the Black Forest and Vosges
were etched sharp on either side of the valley.

And yet, a kind of sadness and dissatisfaction hung about. Still
hangs. The only way to get over it is on.

SILENCE. A SLIGHT STIR overhead to the right. Whip the footstool out of the way to make room for the high reading stand which godo is pulling in front of him. He begins to tell the story of Hyakujo and the fox, adding some thirteenth-century commentary by Dogen. ✓

The question was, If you become a realized, satori-fied person (awake, that is), does the law of karma cease to operate in respect of you or are you still subject to it? In other words, once you have realized, *inter alia,* the relativity, identity, interdependence, and impermanence of all things, including your own ego, are you free of the intentional words and actions and thoughts leading up to you now from the beginning of time (the wars, your education, your nation, your genes, the quarrel you had last night) or are you still subject to their effects?

No right answer, no wrong answer. But yet not so simple as that. Godo leaves out the accretions of centuries. Our master left them out too and simplified, leaning in the direction of *"Fumai! Kuramasanai!"*—Don't try to hide your traces, cover your tracks, escape from the law of karma.

But go all the way to the bottom of your actions—all the way, which means beyond yourself; and it may then be possible to reduce, limit the amount of karma they create; although that is not said in so many words.

ONE MORNING IN MONTREAL I made seventeen phone calls, confirming, altering, adding and eliminating. When I came into the room where everybody was gathered I was probably palpably crackling with electricity and irritation. He shot a sizing-up glance from under heavy lids and, leaving the conversation to eddy on around, grabbed one of my feet and then the other and roughly, brusquely massaged away the telephone calls, one by one, leaving me gasping and grateful on the floor.

What matters is that the whole atmosphere should be in harmony; so what is showing compassion for one jarring energy is also acting in the general interest, or self-interest. They are not separate in the Oriental social code or mentality. We, with our categorizing morality, want to distinguish between compassion and self-interest; but, in fact, no such distinction exists.

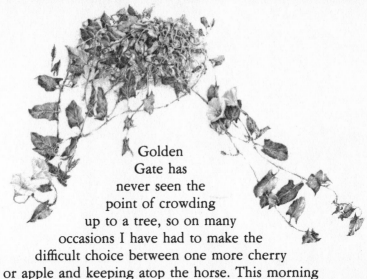

Golden
Gate has
never seen the
point of crowding
up to a tree, so on many
occasions I have had to make the
difficult choice between one more cherry
or apple and keeping atop the horse. This morning
was no exception.

We were coming home through the little vineyard a mile or
less from the stable, a few hundred feet of narrow strips of vines
on the side of the only approximation to a hill, as distinct from the
long sweeps of barely rising, barely falling farmland, in the district.
Situated in the north of Alsace, it is not much good for grapes and
the wines it produces are for home consumption by the farmers and
not entitled to the *appellation.* It is a favorite place of mine, because
so small and amateur. In the autumn, instead of all the industrial
gunk large owners spray over their vines to protect them, the
peasants here hang rabbit skins or crow cadavers on posts, or let off
firecracker pops from time to time, or string shiny bottlecaps between the rows.

As we came along today I stopped at one particular small strip,
two rows of vines wide and maybe sixty feet long, which had been
burned. I don't know whether it was an accident, or a malevolence,
or a deliberate fire to kill infected plants, or what. Anyway it was
very noticeable among the other vines so laden with leaf and heavy
dense clumps of grapes beginning to ripen and color, and so was
the puny tree standing up between the two rows of seared vine

plants. Almost all its leaves had burned and dropped off but there were still a dozen fruits hanging from the thin branches. They looked like peaches. They *were* peaches.

After much coercing and argument and dismounting and remounting I got one, and ate it.

Thinking, For years I have heard people talking about *pêches des vignes,* vine peaches. I have bought them and have eaten them and have found them as they are reputed to be, small and exquisite. I have heard that they grow in vineyards; but that, somehow, I failed to believe. I expect I would have described them to another ignorant foreigner as growing in vineyards but it would have been without conviction because I had looked at a good many vineyards one way and another in France, Germany, Austria and Italy, and had never seen a peach tree in one. I'd have added that such things certainly did not happen in Alsace, however, because peaches, I would have asserted, do not grow so far north except maybe in convent cloisters.

Very often, though not always, that is the way it goes: we half-accept what we are told and transmit it the same—halfway. Then we discover a thing for ourselves and trumpet it out as though nobody had ever discovered it before. It has become real.

The people who are trying to improve educational systems know all about this. So do a lot of other people, I guess: we found it out when we were working on an experimental youth project in London and realized that it was useless for us to consult the records of our predecessors because we couldn't act on what they had learned and useless for us to keep records ourselves because those who came after us would have to learn it all over again; and having realized this we became as cynical toward the university researchers following us around as we had initially been keen to have them, and we, or at least I, also became rather desperate. Shades of Shaw and Methuselah. History clearly has *some* use; but *what?* And *why* should we be unable to profit from others' experience?

A Zen answer would be, Because an experience that is not in your own body-mind is not an experience: you *cannot* know it. And zazen, it would add, is the experience that enables you to have all experiences in one. What Sensei called the cable car direct to the mountaintop.

In every day living, *why* is irrelevant.

The question, how to proceed this being the case, remains.

JEAN SAID, THE MAIN thing is to find out whether you want to live and what for.

I struggled with that, very briefly but eyebrow-to-eyebrow, and announced, a few days later, I don't know what for. I want to live in order to find out what for.

That was a major step. It was also a jolt to find out that I had *absolutely* nothing more to say on the subject.

I read publications of the official cancer association here, in which ovarian cancer was called the silent killer. That gave me a chill.

And somewhere, I read something that said perhaps it is necessary for a person with cancer to accept, in some sense, the cancerous cells, in order for them to become vulnerable or reconvertible into ordinary cells or something to that effect. When I read that I had a "sort of sinking feeling," as it says in children's books, but also something that might have been acquiescence. Another jolt.

I rang my family in the States. My brother rang back and said he was not so hot for chemotherapy because he knew people who'd had it and they weren't around anymore, but he would talk to an internist friend.

I lied to the surgeon and obtained from him an extremely terse report, ostensibly destined for the internist friend of my brother in the States but really for myself.

I rang friends in England and very quickly received a load of information about heat treatments in Australia and the Cancer Self-Help Centre in Bristol—by which I was tempted; it looked like a lot of sense but lacked something, balance or a solid foundation, I don't know. Also a book by one of the top French cancer specialists about the standard medical establishment procedures. I can't say it was boring because there was a fascination about everything I read in those days, but it was weighted down by the same thing I had felt in the clinic and would feel again in the cancer clinic, some unclear relationship with sickness and death in which guilt and remorse and complicity are involved and it is hard to breathe. Something that is profoundly, powerfully wrong.

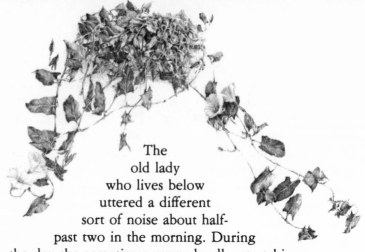

The
old lady
who lives below
uttered a different
sort of noise about half-
past two in the morning. During
the day she sometimes yawns loudly, stretching
her vocal chords the way other people stretch their
backs: a surprising sound, at first, but on the whole a happy one.
This was more like a moan, however, a muffled growl of resistance.
It was repeated.

There has already been one death in the house since we came
here ten years ago, the old man who lived with the woman on the
second floor, and it's on the cards that our neighbor on the third
will go the same way, pretty much in her sleep.

A few more ruminations in this vein, and the seven or eight
church bells within hearing clanged 3 A.M. I realized that I was in
the throes of my first insomnia since before I went into hospital.

The cause, on this occasion, was simply jet lag no doubt. Saturday and Sunday had been merged into one long day-night-day
beginning at ten in the morning on Saturday in Los Angeles and
ending at four on Sunday afternoon in Strasbourg. One unpacked
and sorted the mail and totted up one's bank balance which dis-
agreed violently with one's checkbook and fell into bed Sunday
evening at nine, waking refreshed and with a sense of perfect
readjustment Monday morning to go to work. Apparently, the
sense of readjustment was illusory, however, because there I was
Monday night glaring at the ceiling.

I remembered saying to Jakusho Kwong on Friday night in Los Angeles, after we had thrashed through our cancers at the end of Maezumi Roshi's dinner party, that I had been curiously relieved, when awaiting the results of a scan a year and a half after the original diagnosis, to find myself feeling apprehension once again.

It is true that I had noticed once or twice during those months that I didn't seem to be afraid of anything any more and had wondered about that; there was always the possibility, of course, that one had somehow gone beyond fear but I rather doubted it, and thought it more likely that I had put up some sort of buffer to cover the duration of the mobilization and make it possible for me to keep the whole unwieldy therapeutic process in motion. And it is true too that I almost welcomed, or at least recognized with the mildly affectionate tolerance one shows to the pet dog of some seldom-seen casual friend, the spasm of dread that shot through me when one or another of the doctors I have seen in the last few weeks spoke of the likelihood of recurrence.

But as I lay quarreling last night with my insomnia, that comment to Jakusho struck me as literary, fatuous, irresponsible and in bad taste. It still does this morning, in a heavy autumn Alsatian rain. The dominant element at the moment, however, is real grogginess. Plain punch-drunk, I am, hovering between surliness and tears, and as unwilling to face the work on my desk as a child kept in class after school and about to write for the sixty-seventh time (out of one hundred), "I must not make rude noises behind the teacher's back."

SILENCE. THE REMARKable quality of silence when 220 people are highly concentrated without any conscious effort of will; a silence that is a roaring blaze, and also nothing at all. The quality of silence that has produced all those tales about monks who were manifestly not there when robbers came to kill them and those images of forests of ebony and old, dried, cliff-hung pines.

"Kai-jo": open the meditation. Feet pad over the carpet. Sound of a lighter being held to candles and incense at the altar. Nine loud thumps on the big drum tell the hour. A pause; from the dining hall across the little stream outside, a clang, metal against metal, saying: the food is ready. Another; another; a roll of accelerating clangs; a second roll; then a single clang, followed by a sharp thock on the gaetan just outside the dojo—wood against wood, answering: the dojo is ready—then alternating with the kitchen metal in a third roll. Three final strokes, and 220 voices ring out the kesa sutra, with kesa or rakusu folded on their heads.

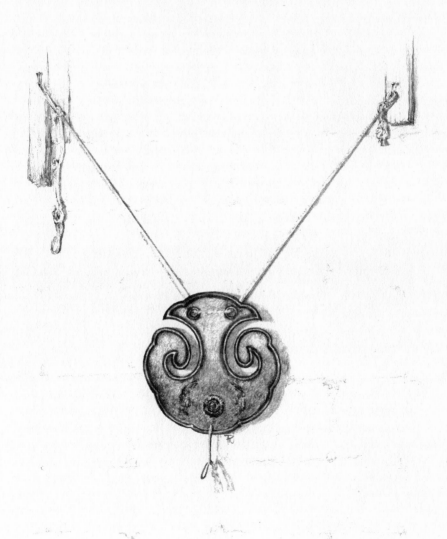

the metal

Perhaps
things will
settle down now.
There were those three
weeks in the States, Jean's
first trip. What can I say about
them?

Well, Ben-Gay exists. You may have to go to
the Farmer's Store in Chetek, Wisconsin, population 1,931, to find
it; but it's there.

There was a week back here, getting ready for the sesshin in
Lausanne.

There was the sesshin in Lausanne.

Well? Well?

The saying in me seems to have dried up.

Jean and the cat and the horse and the fish and the garden (and
the office) are all here, October is thinning into November. There
is a great deal to be done and although the world is falling about
our ears I can find no reason not to begin.

THE HIRED CAR PULLED up to the curb on the Canadian side of the Falls. It was late afternoon, cold and gray and a lashing wind. I opened the door, Sensei hopped out and strode ahead of us to the railing over the water. When I got there he said, looking at Niagara, "All my life I think about see Niagara Falls but I never believe I come here. Now I here."

His bounding delight expended itself in hours of poring over junk in the souvenir shop and acquiring a motley assortment of it for family, friends and disciples.

A SINGLE STROKE OF THE gong; people stand and range themselves in lines along the sides. Godo walks forward to the altar.

Move to the mat in the center, unfold his zagu, retreat to position behind on his left, unfold own zagu, three prosternations, sit, and the ceremony gong announces the *Hannya Shingyo,* chanted three times vigorously at a good (and increasing) clip to the sound of the wooden fish, joined for the second and third repetitions by the big drum. Irresistible streams of energy pour out and away. The vows are chanted and the closing invocation. Godo bows to everyone and says good morning.

mokugyo, the wooden fish whose eyes are never closed

drum

I took
my saddle
and the double
bridle home to clean
and oil last night. The
bridle doesn't get cleaned nearly
often enough, which means that I don't know
how to reassemble it automatically and must go through
the same performance each time—and I begin it, each time, with
the same daredevil offhandedness. I suppose this is a challenge, to
see whether I have grown more stupid in the months intervening,
or whether some parts of the process have become second nature.
In any event, after dinner and washing the dishes to clear a space
on the counter, I begin by observing that one strap is fastened in
the third hole on the right side and in the fourth on the left and
deciding that it will never be possible to remember them all in the
right order, and then proceed to dismantle the bridle as though it
were burning my fingers and fling all the separate parts of it to the
floor in gay abandon.

I then wash the bits, scraping and scratching away at incrusta-
tions of saliva and straw that become enamel-hard over the months
(this is only in corners and at edges, I do actually rinse the bits
daily). There is always a terrible struggle to prize the leather curb-
strap loose and detach its two parts from the rings, and the barely
mastered panic that I will never be able to reassemble them again
because their buckles and tag-ends fit together more nonsensically
than any Chinese puzzle and although I have ultimately succeeded
in putting them back the way they were before every time I have

cleaned the bridle in the five years I have had it, I have never been sure I put it together right the first time.

I usually leave that till the end but this time I did it first, before patience was worn to a frazzle, and after trying only three or four combinations found what seemed to be the way they go. I have often uttered a grunt of triumph over the curb-strap only to find that I had forgotten to thread the curb-chain through it beforehand but this time, again, I got it right.

Then there are all the cheek-straps, noseband, headband, browband and two pairs of reins to wash, dry and oil. With neat's-foot oil. I often wonder about the manufacturers of neat's-foot oil. I have seen only one brand, ever, and think it may be a monopoly, at least in England and on the Continent. Is there enough demand for neat's-foot oil to make one man extremely rich? Is his factory huge, with hundreds of employees, or is it a shed at the back of his house? Is there a mountain of cattle bones piled in the yard or do they come from the slaughterhouse packed in rows? Are you a neat's-foot oil manufacturer from father to son?

Then, slowly, remembering that the wider reins go with the snaffle bit and the narrower ones with the curb, that there are three buckles on the left side but only one on the right, putting the browband around your own forehead and almost feeling ears prick up the sides of your head to hold it in place, observing with fumbling amazement how necessary and justified each intricate part is and how, if you make a mistake, the anatomy of the horse's head shows you at once that what you have done is impossible, you put it all back together again, and at the end survey the result with a feeling of pity for the poor beast with all that weight of metal in its mouth, mixed with respect for the power of the beast that makes all that weight of metal necessary if you want to have any control over it, and with admiration for the human cunning that devised this means of exerting not just brute control but such precise control as can be obtained, with very little strength, by means of a double bridle—and for the human intention or ideal, which was to achieve, starting from the lump of bone and muscle and confusion that we are and the bulk of bone and muscle and fright that is the horse, the light, compact, cadenced futility of the dressage horse and rider moving through their circles and figures, ample yet spare, every fiber in a balance of opposing and converging forces and energies yet demonstrating the essence of free motion.

And I thought, when the bridle was back together again, that through some similar process it will be possible to move forward from the shambles in our sangha left by the sudden death, intestate in every sense of the word, of our master.

I WAS IN TOUCH WITH AN-
other homeopathic doctor in
Rouen, through one of Jean's
sons in Paris. He made helpful
noises but was a long way away.

Everybody was a long way
away. I did not know where to
look for what I seemed to be
going to need very badly, an ordinary family doctor who would
know about things and be able to discuss them. I never found one,
and in the end ran my own show—medically. In every other respect
I hope it is clear that I was surrounded by the finest possible sup-
port.

I went to the cancer clinic for a first meeting with the head
chemotherapist and husband of my terrifying anesthetist. We took
violently against each other at first sight. I tried to get over that by
making jokes to friends about their married life.

I saw a top surgeon in town who had taken care of a good
friend of mine; he tut-tutted genially and said he had a friend at
another hospital who was not averse to combining treatments, even
including the mistletoe for instance, but the friend was a radiologist
and not a chemotherapist.

One evening I went to have dinner with some very close
friends, one of whom had long been a disciple of Sensei's before
going back to work to bring up his kids. He met me at the door,
slung an arm round my shoulders and wisecracked, Good karma,
huh? Brings you close to the Way.

The jolt I felt then showed me very clearly that I had been
thinking, Bad karma. Within a fraction of a second the molecules
turned themselves round and reorganized. I am flatly grateful to
him forever.

I sat in zazen pretty regularly, and one evening there was an obscure movement—of molecules, I say again, not knowing really what it is that moves—that had to do with my relationship to my mother, our uneasy inability to unhook from each other, and with my own refusal to have children, and in which floated the concluding sentence of a tiny French book by an ex-Lacanian woman analyst about mother-daughter relationships; the sentence is something like, If only I could live without your having to die. Yet another jolt, but less sharp and sudden.

I relate all this because it shows what kind of a process I followed, which was haphazard but on all fronts at once. I would recommend it.

It was very hard work; absorbing the jolts no doubt used up a lot of energy but was not perceptibly difficult. What was difficult, and I suppose useful, was making myself pick up the telephone and follow up leads, argue for appointments in two weeks' time when you were told that you could have none within three months, talk to recording devices, insist, reserve a seat on a plane and tickets on trains.

It took two weeks.

Those
few times
in October and
November when it was
possible to get to the
stable and out, there was a peculiar
reluctance, dis-taste.

The autumn was quietly superb to look at,
although its colors were more muted even than usual here in Alsace, where they never begin to equal the assertiveness of those in
the States. Yet every leaf had done its utmost, even if it was still
almost wholly green, with only the edge dried to dun and a narrow
strip of yellow running round behind.

When Jacques the calligrapher was here after Lausanne he
took some petals falling from the last roses on the rose tree and
calligraphed them, and one or two large leaves from my hamamelis
that had turned a clear, bright yellow. André gathered them,
Jacques calligraphed them, I dried them, Nicole and Marianne
mounted them, Hughes gave them away at the sesshin here last
week. They were lovely.

And forgotten.

Sensei said one time, The journey is so much more beautiful
than the arrival.

The rest of the hamamelis leaves looked as though they meant
to stick fast again this year. Last year they never fell at all, perhaps
because the autumn was so mild, so this year I detached them one
by one, gingerly, hoping the tree would forgive my meddling
aesthetic sense. Because in January, the first week in January (the

last two years it's been exactly on the seventh, but that no doubt was because the temperature happened to be above freezing on the seventh), the hamamelis suddenly flowers, tousled bright yellow blossoms with bits of rusty red, even in two feet of snow; and the sight is so heartening and gay that I don't want it hidden by leftover leaves.

So: what was—as one rode the emptying fields, a quick third crop of hay here and there, the corn coming down bit by bit, winter wheat germinating and poking above the surface, partridge now and then, an odd pheasant or hare, the larks starting up in their little flocks, and the chaffinches, tits on their rounds in the forest, and the larger and larger flights of pigeons and gulls and rooks and crows, growing year by year, the birds that thrive on us, battening upon the ploughed empty fields in hundreds and rising raggedly from time to time, the rooks like clockwork leaving their rookeries at dawn and flying over the city alongside the cathedral and out to the fields to poke and prowl and sit, and back again at dusk, a dense chattering intimate presence overhead in the blank gray morning, in the gathering gray night; then only the cabbages left and soil-enricher crops to harvest in the spring, and then row by row in the small hand-worked fields, strip by strip in the big machine-farmed fields, the cabbages cut from their stalks and knocked to one side, then forked or picked up by machines and lobbed into big wagons, then driven to the cooperative where the conveyor belt of the ramp turns all day long, the cabbage heads disappearing on one side and their outside leaves trundling up to the top of the belt on the other side and plopping into the empty wagon below, to be driven back to the fields and scattered and spread as fertilizer, and then the first frost, a few more days of thin sunlight, then hard frost and this morning every twig coated with hoar, every car and window and roof, and the sky not fog or cloud but a blank colorless spread of suspended frost—what was this dis-taste?

Had one seen too many autumns? God, no. Had the summer

been too beautiful and was one dreading its end? No, it had been beautiful and one was ready for a change. One had nothing against autumn, one was not tired of it. And if it didn't seem to be showing much that was new, that was one's own fault because one wasn't really looking. Far down, preoccupied was what one was.

RUN TO PICK UP HIS ZAGU, collect papers from reading stand, push through the crowd coming out, shove on sandals, stagger after godo and bell-girl who are already halfway to the tomb mound, followed by the ceremony boy carrying a fancy itinerant incense-burner used when people are touring around and have to stop and burn incense in front of every altar or holy place they see. Godo's new toy.

On the mound, while the others are performing their bows and incense-burnings, see a straw-colored meadow behind the oak trunks come to life as the sun clears the morning clouds.

Rush to godo's room, pick up bowls, follow the procession round the back of the main building and down to the kitchen, exchanging greetings, information, gossip, orders of the day.

Between kitchen and dining room, another run through the *Hannya Shingyo*, this time at top speed, to the racing *ting-a-ling*s of the bell-girl.

File down the dining room to the end table, deposit bowls on table in front of godo and accoutrements on small table behind, rush around table to seat opposite godo as the big wooden clappers resound to begin meal sutra.

And
what of
Jacob? To whom
this writing is also
dedicated.
Perhaps I must leave it at
that. There are too many hundreds of thousands
of young lives brutally cut off, for his to be anything
special.

I have written several things about him and thrown them away. Every word implies too many others.

He was killed, run over by a truck in London, not so long after Sensei's death; and as much as Sensei's death left a world complete and work to be done, Jacob's death left nothing. Left me stuck.

The world is full of mothers and lovers getting over deaths, going beyond them, going on, getting up in the morning and putting kettles on to boil. Being towers of strength, or pillars, or whichever phallic word it is.

Zen tends rather to favor strength, and has little or no time for weakness and mourning and missing. But there was a moment, unexpected and absolutely poignant, at a sesshin one summer in Val d'Isère when Sensei was trying to teach us about karma and had to refer to the Indian antecedents of Chinese and Japanese Buddhism, which meant that he had to deal with death and reincarnation. ("The end is the end. More we cannot know. Perhaps something lives on. Zen has nothing to say about metaphysical matters.") When suddenly there was a kind of hole, a change of key or register, and he was speaking privately, as if to himself, of his first secretary in France, a young woman killed in a car crash. Clearly, he was stuck too.

"I do not know if I shall see her again, meet somewhere, after I die. But"—and his voice went a little thin and almost self-conscious—"I hope. I hope."

There is more than one chain leading us into the past and connecting, more than just tradition, or history, or genetics, or the ironic points of light that flash out in art and literature: there are also hands held across silence.

I FLEW DOWN TO SEE THE man in the south of France. From Nice I had quite a few miles to go and took a bus along the coast, the awful, mucked-about, overcrowded, gorgeous coast. It was not the season, and "season" people don't take buses much, and I felt wonderfully solid and firm among the  local mixed-blood people going up or down the line a few stops, North African, Provençal-Italian, and the retired Americans and English already suffering from April heat, diffident about themselves because they equate their age and decrepitude with unimportance and are at the same time firmly committed to their eccentricities of dress or behavior. It was a great bus ride, nobody was in a hurry or could be and nothing was more or less than itself. The sea was blue. The beaches empty.

The doctor useful. Do your chemotherapy, he said, because the protocols they're using nowadays for ovarian cancer look pretty good; but do the following as well. And he gave me a long list of things to do at once and later, consisting chiefly of injections lasting over an hour of a mixture of highly non-toxic, almost old-fashioned substances meant to support liver and kidneys, and vitamin C and trace elements. Tests to have before each chemotherapy period, called Vernes cancerometry tests—they had to be read in Paris, which meant more complicated businesses of getting samples taken, packaging them and sending them by post oneself. The injections were to be done by a nurse who would come to the house. (Find her.) There were also things to take that had to be ordered from Switzerland because they were taboo in France. Some I ordered and used, others not. It was a matter of what I fancied or didn't fancy.

The next morning in Blois (Sensei had died that night in

Tokyo) the diet-iridologist-Oriental diagnosis man said, Do your chemotherapy and we'll see afterward. He gave me a very detailed diet including sketches of a knife point with "that much" fermented soybean paste on it.

I had liked both these men and they had both said, Do your chemotherapy and we'll see and had been businesslike about what else I should do. I made up my mind to do it.

THE NIGHT WE LANDED at O'Hare there were several conventions in Chicago. Three hotel rooms for four people had been booked, with some difficulty; but we were seven. That morning, by telephone from Toronto, I had finally contrived to book a couple of rooms very far north in the suburbs, almost to Wisconsin. It meant splitting up. I tried to hire two cars but there were no cars of any description to be hired in the whole of Chicago, by any company, at any price. I found out about public transport to the northern suburb and took tickets for the three extra people.

I did all this very quickly because Sensei did not like to sit around in airports; then I joined the others, surrounded by suitcases in the evacuation-of-Warsaw atmosphere of that crazy place.

I explained the arrangements. He disliked separations. He started working something out in his mind. "What rooms like in hotel?" he asked. I don't know, I told him. "Ask," he said.

Gawdalmighty, I thought, imagining how the request was going to be treated by a hotel clerk facing a line of seventy-six conventioneers clamoring for their rooms. And I hate telephoning from airports and using coins and not having enough and the noise. As I turned away to telephone, I felt something yield, stretch.

The clerk was extremely polite. I reported back. Sensei worked it out that we could all manage in the three rooms except the seventh person who might have to sleep on the floor. (In the end he didn't even.)

That is what he was so good at: inventing ways out that were always ways beyond, and educating—literally drawing out, stretching—his disciples at the same time: getting them to make a swimming pool full of children be quiet because zazen is going on next door, or the French air force schedule its flights overhead between zazens, or the workmen in the street start drilling later and put silencers on their drills, or a crew of young men to spend six or eight months building at La Gendronnière on twenty dollars a month (and then losing his temper when they threatened to strike if he didn't buy them a washing machine); making people resourceful and self-reliant, unknown to themselves, in a world peopled increasingly by dependent sheep and rabbits and a few equally dependent bullies.

It's
pretty bleak
out these days.
Ground either just-
freezing or just unfreezing,
a powder of snow fringing roofs and
edging pockmarks in the earth, an uninterested
sky, water steaming but not quite freezing where
there is a current, ducks and swans and coots paddling aimlessly in
disorderly smudges, blackbirds plunging from perch to perch with
an effortful choppy wing-stroke, and the ever-present swirl of pigeons and rooks over the fields.

However, the press of medical alarums and excursions and
routine duties is such that sometimes a trot over even these inhospitable furrows comes as a relief.

On days when the ground is not stone-hard and one is not
condemned to work in the indoor ring in careful circles, avoiding
other riders while making unrewarding comparisons between their
mounts and seats and techniques and one's own, I stand in the stable
courtyard thinking which direction to take, and none is more alluring than any other. Except that the forest seems to hold out a slight
promise of warmth, or absence of positive cold. It is now entirely
forbidden to us but I go there occasionally even so.

It can be lovely. Silent. Quickly the silence spreads round, one
is like a fish swimming through a water of silence. And then in parts
of the forest there is a patchwork of plantings, a stand of beech,
several hundred yards of straight thick trunks with no undergrowth; and ash, and then mixed pines and fir, then dense Scotch

pine planted for quick crops, below which nothing lives; then oak with a few self-sown birch and alder and a wild cherry now and then. Trotting through them is a pleasure, the speed is just right, the height is right, you have them just as long as your eye needs them, a scarf of green a scarf of black a scarf of beige a scarf of gray-silver a scarf of dun.

The tits call now and then, and you see one flip up, bright against the subtle old tones of the bark, and snicker off to another tree. You are intimate with every living thing in the forest, the cold walls you in with each bird or tree trunk you see. Sometimes, suddenly, you hear the insane blare of the loggers' saw. Then you drop back to a walk and listen. Having already paid one large fine, you do not want to be caught.

Which direction? How far away? You peer through the woods for a curl of smoke from their fire. You creep up to crossings and ease your neck around corners, preparing to head off at a gallop in the opposite direction at the sight of another human. You rise in the stirrups and shade your eyes with a hand, and realize that you are playing, in dead earnest and high glee, cowboys and Indians again.

BIG BOWLS OF GEN MAI
are brought up at the end of the
first verse of the meal sutra.

Gen Mai

For 100 people:

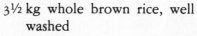

3½ kg whole brown rice, well
    washed
2 kg carrots
1 kg turnips
1 kg celery (or celeriac)
2 kg leeks

Wash and brush vegetables, do not manhandle. Other vegetables
can be used (not onions), but this is a good combination. Soak rice
twelve hours. Vegetables should be cut or diced very finely indeed.
After soaking, brown the rice very gently in large pan or the bottom
of cooking vessel, without oil, stirring constantly. Then cook it,
covered, in eight times or more its volume of water, pouring water
cold on top of the rice, for two hours. Vegetables can be browned
separately, covered, over a low flame, also stirring regularly, but in
a tiny amount of oil, or simply in the water still on them from
washing. Add vegetables to rice and cook another hour and a half
at least, covered. Use no salt, pepper or spices. Serve with gomasio
(sesame seed and salt in varying proportions, lightly grilled and
ground in a mortar) and tamari.

    The cook is the second most important person in the commu-
nity, and by his gen mai is he known. Once you're used to it, it can
make your day.

    This is a thick gen mai, in which carrots and leeks and other
vegetables have cooked for hours and hours in brown rice, a gen
mai that is probably thicker and richer than was ever consumed in
the temples of China or Japan in the old days.

    Well, at least there'll be one real recipe in this book.

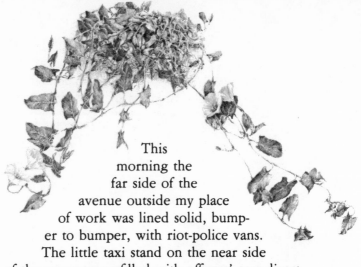

This
morning the
far side of the
avenue outside my place
of work was lined solid, bumper to bumper, with riot-police vans.
The little taxi stand on the near side
of the avenue was filled with officers' cars direct-
ing operations. The side street was lined with more vans of riot
police. The bank of the river beyond the main building was lined
with snazzy modern tanks or some other lethal machine. At every
pathway into the municipal park across from the office building
stood heavily beweaponed blue men, and there were more of them
at every street corner busily snarling traffic out of their way; there
were motor-rafts full of uniforms skidding up and down the river
and canal and sending the winter flocks of ducks and grebes and
swans and coots and moorhens into panicky circles. Why haven't we
seen any helicopters yet?

This afternoon the situation is exactly the same, except that
there are even more chunks of blue biped meat hulking about the
corners.

All this is on account of a demonstration of winegrowers who
want to petition the European Parliament about something.

There were rumored to be 2,500 of them heading for Strasbourg. I wonder if anybody has seen a single one. There must be
at least two law-and-orders for every demonstrator, wherever they
are. And wherever they are, I hope they're warm.

The riot police do not look warm. They look red in the face, cross and menacing. They look supremely silly, too, in the placid landscape of a moderately-to-highly-inefficient, moderately pretentious international organization in a medium-sized provincial European town. If they were all screaming and doing bloody battle with enraged winegrowers they would still look silly, but also terrifying. So far there have been no operations for their officers to direct. There has been nothing.

Makes you wonder about living in a democracy. One way and another, there's as much manipulation and overkill there as elsewhere.

Democracy my foot. Just past the last of the tanks there is an advertisement pillar covered in posters for *Swan Lake,* the holiday season's ballet offering, and other posters for I don't know what in which the word *liberté* figures prominently.

Not that the winegrowers are sinless. I am told, and believe, that table wine in France and elsewhere in the Common Market has deteriorated very substantially of late. Since I stopped drinking it I've lost my taste, however, and plonk and Vosne-Romanée are all the abominably same to me.

But what idiocy! One leaning tower of illusion–ego attachments glaring at another leaning tower of illusion–ego attachments.

We are often—nay constantly, I am tempted to say—flummoxed and exasperated by conflicting pressures of this sort, leading to expostulations and vehemence, of this sort and worse.

Do not get stuck in the illusion of contradiction, of duality, taught Sensei. Lean neither to left nor to right, neither backwards nor forwards. Embrace all contradictions and create, go forward, go beyond. Exactly like the zazen posture.

One doesn't always have the true creative intuition, however, so one does the best one can. For me that often means a gratuitous act, a gesture, art-for-art's-sake. In this instance, irritated by the irrelevance of a pitched battle between thousands of para-military and thousands of protesting winegrowers as a means of regulating the problems of the European wine market, my own response is suddenly to offer to do a piece of work for nothing, because various parties are bickering about how much to pay for it.

Sensei also said, "I am a Zen monk and cannot talk about politics. If you follow me I shall teach you why it is better to avoid politics." He took an equally dim view of journalism and theater —I presume because those professions are consecrations of lies. Journalism I could see, about theater I didn't agree (he was himself an excellent actor; maybe that had something to do with it) and always meant to ask him but never got around to it.

I followed; and have learned that it is better to avoid politics —preferences, choosing, egotisms, power—but would find myself hard put to say *why,* in terms any active member of the citizenry would understand. I must work on that.

But then he said, "You must not run away from the world on the ground that you are a monk. You must know what is happening in the world." Really know. Not the epiphenomena, the day's events; but the movements of societies, the big discoveries. And really not choose.

A very different matter from sitting groggily in front of the television, exclaiming over turpitudes and ineptitudes and shedding tears or uttering imprecations over catastrophes and inhumanities and going off to open another can of beer.

So: not choosing involves a fair amount of choice. This is not a contradiction.

I SAID SOME PAGES BACK that one day I must remember to write about how one thing does not lead to another. Here are a few, possibly cryptic words on the subject:

I mixed my cocktail, thus, and I stuck to it. Doubts I had, and have, but they are foam in the brain. What I knew, and not just in the brain, was that you don't make deals with life-and-death.

It isn't: if I am a good girl I'll get a piece of candy and a pat on the head. If I take my pills and injections and eat my rice and vegetables I'll live forever and not die of cancer. It isn't that. It's: as long as I'm living I'll live. When I'm dying I'll die.

Everything is interdependent, so your pills and injections and rice and vegetables do have to do with your state of health. But you can't blame them if you die anyway. That is how, oddly enough, one thing does not lead to another.

FROM ST. LOUIS TO New Orleans the plane was almost empty. There might have been fifteen passengers in all. Immediately after takeoff the five of us spread all over it, each taking a window seat on the right side of the plane. The Mississippi wound complicatedly underneath and the setting sun remained almost motionless as we flew south, out and away from the Pole toward the bulge. The bands of earth's atmosphere were sharply marked and intense.

Nobody spoke to anybody. Everybody sat and stared out the window. That gap, those hours shared on that airplane with the red sun not managing to go down—

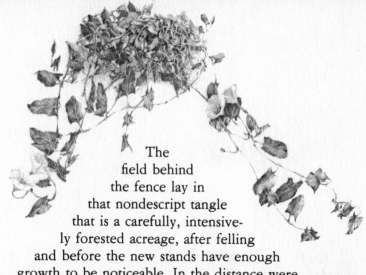

The
field behind
the fence lay in
that nondescript tangle
that is a carefully, intensive-
ly forested acreage, after felling
and before the new stands have enough
growth to be noticeable. In the distance were
conifers two feet high needing protection from the roe deer; the
rest, newly planted in oak, seemed to be all twigs and tufts of dried
frosted weed, lengths of useless branch, an occasional sickly birch,
a few wild alders, stumps of big trees felled and removed a few
years back, now disappearing under weeds and moss, newer stumps
still showing saw marks but their color beginning to yellow, clumps
of fern gone brown, strands of honeysuckle torn from their support-
ing limbs and dangling, a few leaves still green clinging to them;
over all the powder of frost and light snow, a troubled, yellow,
afternoon sky with a tiny patch of blue in one corner but mostly
snow-bearing cloud partly advancing, partly hovering, uncertain.
No wind, no sound.

Golden Gate swung to a halt and twisted his head back over
his left shoulder.

The hen harrier was quartering the field, methodical, low-
flying, a large pale blue-gray body and wings with dramatic black
fingers at the tips, now stroking now gliding, stroking and gliding,
turning and crossing. After a minute she flew to a clear spot among
the baby conifers and settled on the ground.

Golden Gate resumed his hurried trot homeward.

EACH PERSON HAS A PRIvate ritual for gen mai. Some want only a teaspoonful, others want their bowl filled to the brim, some put masses of gomasio on top, others none at all, some pour tamari in the bottom of the bowl before the gen mai is added, others splash it on afterward. But at the end of the sutra when the bowls are raised in front of the faces, spoon facing out, they are all pretty much at the same height.

Eat in silence. Listen to announcements. Make list in head of people to see and things to do. Chant closing sutra, pick up bits and pieces and walk back to godo's room in main building—a minute off duty if he hasn't beckoned. The morning is clearing and will be hot, but the late summer flowers alongside the dojo look pretty sad.

THE NEXT MEETING WITH
the head of chemotherapy at the
cancer clinic was something
else. I said I wanted to see my
file, that I was legally entitled to
see it; he said, Send me your
lawyer and I'll send you mine. I
said I would be doing *a, b* and
c alongside his treatment and
perhaps he would like to take

that into account, and he said he would not begin his treatment until
I promised him I was doing nothing at all alongside it. Whereupon
I said, I promise, and laughed, and he spluttered at what he read
as my bad faith.

He talked to me at some length about his responsibility, and
I said, I'm forty-seven years old, if I'm not a little bit responsible
for myself now I never will be. When he heard about the diet and
other things he said, in the tones of offense and disapproval I
associate with a university professor discussing an error of reason-
ing in a term paper—offense and disapproval and condemnation
without appeal—, You're making Pascal's wager (Pascal who said,
Get down on your knees and pray and faith will follow—and after
all, it *might* be true), and I said, You bet I am.

I'm religious, I added. That was not the word I would have
chosen if I had been talking to someone who might understand but
it seemed to be the word closest to what I thought might be his
vocabulary; and he shut up and stared, and then snorted a little and
shrugged.

Of course, the man is desperately hard-working, and conscien-
tious, and why should he have to put up with a stroppy foreign
woman who is half threatening to make public trouble for him?

He did try to wriggle out of it at one point, saying, Why don't
you go somewhere else? I don't really want to treat you here, but

when I answered, Because I have decided to have the course of chemotherapy and your hospital is the best-equipped in this region, you are specialists and your techniques are the most up-to-date and I am asking you to do your job, he found nothing to counter with, but it was clearly hard for him to match that with Pascal's wager and what he associated with "I'm religious."

He is part of the something I felt in those clinics that I call wrong. He didn't want just to be obeyed; he wanted, I think, to be trusted or loved or forgiven. I later saw him deploying floods of gentleness and consideration with women who were resigned and suffering, dying, in fact. And there was trust or love or forgiveness involved, I think. But there is a hypocrisy at the bottom of it, an evasion, that I don't put my finger on and it is terrible.

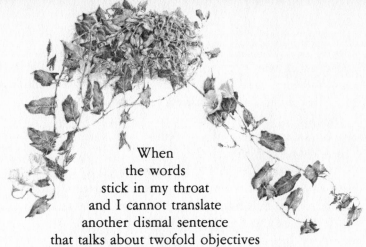

When
the words
stick in my throat
and I cannot translate
another dismal sentence
that talks about twofold objectives
and development cooperation, when the mind
blanks out in front of the year-in-year-out repetition
of texts most of which have been sincerely written by people who
are not wholly fools, when mental indigestion reaches retching
level, and I am afraid that means often, I look out the window. I
have colleagues more disciplined than I who resolutely turn their
typewriters or dictaphones to the wall, and beneath the mild con-
tempt I entertain for them as half-dead and soulless lies humble
admiration, for they are all busy building homes and raising families
and contributing to valid charities and singing in choirs and studying more languages and doing aerobics.

I, meanwhile, when not rereading old-fashioned detective stories, waste my time looking out the window.

And every day I see beautiful French military aircraft coming
down to land, often in close formation with what look like inches
between the planes; by these I am grudgingly impressed. Less often,
but regularly in autumn and winter, I see swans, alone or in couples
and sometimes larger flocks, also coming down to land, on the little
river that runs just past the window, northeast-southwest and parallel to the flight lane; by these I am wholeheartedly impressed.

But when, as this morning, I see them together, superimposed,
following exactly parallel angles of descent with their long necks

stretched in front and their wings, steel and feathered alike, set well back and low, I am at a loss. Between natural grace and ingeniousness and human ingeniousness and design, there is no nook or cranny of separation. When there is clearly so much in our works and days that is harmonious, it often seems simply bewildering that there is so much that is not.

Sensei said, Look behind the words to the meaning. Look behind the swans to the meaning of the swans, look behind the planes to the meaning of the planes. And then, look behind that again; and in the end, go back to work.

ARRIVE. REMOVE AND fold kesa in a green-room atmosphere of others doing the same before they sit down to light a cigarette.

Tie back outer sleeves, pound upstairs, pour coffee into big thermos, put a match under pan containing second batch of coffee, back downstairs, start serving and handing out cups, listening, taking occasional part in conversation, answer questions, ask one or two. When most people have left, grab up godo's spare white kimono that was washed in the machine with the kitchen towels after a lunch of mackerel and now smells strongly of fish, upstairs to big bathroom, have a pee, rewash kimono by hand in good soap and hang from a tree outside to dry in sun.

Back to small sitting room to clear cups and saucers and take up to helper who will wash. Prepare two more lots of coffee for after-lunch meeting of heads of provincial and foreign dojos. Give list of things to buy to errand girl.

HIS INTUITION STRUCK AGAIN in New Orleans. While we were unpacking in the hotel rooms, he picked up the local magazine and started looking for a Japanese restaurant. I was dubious, on the grounds that New Orleans had French food and seafood but not Japanese food, but from a group of three or four he poked a finger at a perfectly commonplace advertisement and said, "That one." The taxi was ordered and we set out. It was so far from the center of town that I became increasingly dubious and when we got to it, it looked like any other roadside pseudo-anything restaurant in America.

Inside, however, was another story. It was a big place and almost empty. It had a menu, all in Japanese, the size of a small book, and although the waiter, whom Sensei rightly guessed as Korean, didn't know what it all meant he was able to take the order. Sensei was so glad to see it that he ordered half the things on the menu; and when the waiter got to the kitchen there must have been something of a flurry. The owner appeared, bowing. He knew about Sensei, had read about him in a Japanese newspaper, was honored, bowed some more.

Nobody could eat a quarter of all that food and it somehow became our fault that so much had been ordered. Never mind; the Korean waiter made little animals for us out of bits of paper and the owner had his picture taken with Sensei and presented him with a fat white china Buddha with a hole in its belly for incense.

I was custodian of the hat. The hat was Sensei's Russian sable cap bought in Moscow during a stopover on a flight to Tokyo; he was fiercely attached to it. It made him look entirely absurd. There was also the cape, a huge, heavy black woolen cape made for European winters and the cold we had just come from in Canada. Both were irrelevant in New Orleans, which is on the latitude of Cairo. As we got into the taxi to go back to town Sensei gave me the white china Buddha to hold along with cape and hat, and said, "Do not lose!" I concentrated so hard on not losing the statuette that when we got out of the taxi at the edge of the Vieux Carré I left the hat behind.

The taxi door was hardly shut when he said, "Where hat?"

Gasp. The secretary and I set off at a fast run, on spike-heeled boots, after the taxi vanishing in the distance—for once there was no traffic jam.

A hefty black woman eased out of the darkness and asked, "Anything the matter?" We told her. A little disappointed, I think, by the dimensions and subject matter of the crisis, she nevertheless asked what the taxi looked like and for a wonder, we remembered. "Oh, that'll be one of Geezer's cabs," she said. We went back to the hotel and I got on the phone to Geezer, whose cabs fortunately had radios. The taxi was located and the hat was still in it.

I left some money in an envelope and gave earnest instructions to the hotel desk.

The next morning I raced to the desk, where there was a new shift on duty. At first nobody knew anything about a hat; but eventually, after some coaxing and the kind of tedious perseverance that sometimes gets results, the hat was produced. Clearly, somebody had earmarked it for himself; also, I have no idea if the money ever got to the driver. When I triumphantly placed the hat on the breakfast table Sensei hardly glanced at it and went on talking.

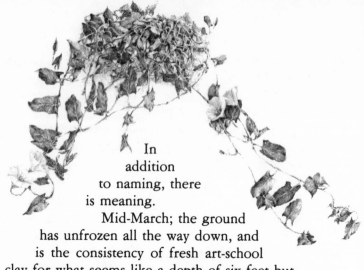

In
addition
to naming, there
is meaning.
Mid-March; the ground
has unfrozen all the way down, and
is the consistency of fresh art-school
clay for what seems like a depth of six feet but
is probably more like eight inches. All squish and goo and sludge,
pulling at the horse's hooves, clutching and at the same time slip-
pery, treacherous and horrible but also rather beautiful, if your face
is not being pushed into it. A tan with silver in it, and black, and
sand, rather like some kinds of chocolate when melted and worked
with butter.

This afternoon, in light, fine rain with golden fans of sunrays
behind it and the blue line of the Vosges very blue on the horizon,
suddenly the air was full of insects flying in circles, going nowhere,
incongruous when there are still crusts of ice along the edges of
ditches and at the bottom of furrows where the sun doesn't strike.
Insects, already! was my response.

A little later, a brace of partridge squirted up underneath the
horse's feet and whirred away. Partridge, nice! was my response.

Then, at the bottom of the same loaf of hill that was all cabbage
knobs last autumn, I looked up and suddenly there were eight deer
profiled against the sky. They bounded quickly out of sight. Eight
at once, I thought, it's as many years since I've seen so large a
group. And then: what does it *mean*?

I invented explanations, some of which I liked and others I

disliked, and soon found myself worrying. And then I thought, The thing about meaning is that it is so tied up with wanting. If you do not care whether the deer flourish and multiply or become extinct then you do not worry about the meaning of eight of them at once, as being a good sign or possibly a bad one. Does anything mean anything, when there is no desire attached to it?

And if you abandon desire, and with it meaning, what do you have? Paragraphs two, three, and four above.

Is that a satisfactory state of affairs, or indeed a possible one? Perhaps.

But like all words, those are incomplete. They sound rather nihilistic—what I used to think Buddhism was, and meditation and so forth, thirty years ago when they were seeping into the diligent New England self-consciousness in which I was being trained, from the decadent West Coast where things were going (fascinatingly, mysteriously) to hell.

I can complete the words, a little. Take "care": you can care enormously whether the deer flourish or become extinct and devote a lot of energy to forwarding one or other of those finalities or some third one, and in that case things have meaning, yes; but you do not "worry" about their meaning. Things can mean, all right, with or without desire. What matters is the "attached to it." If you are not attached to the desire, then the meaning can be clear, and you can be clear. It is the attachment that makes worry, and the worry that makes muddle.

So the end should read, "And if you abandon desire, and with it meaning, what do you have? Paragraphs two, three, and four above. If you abandon attachment to desire, what do you have? Paragraphs two, three, and four above, enriched with meaning and endless possibility for action."

Is that a satisfactory state of affairs, or indeed a possible one?

AT 10:30, WHEN BONSHO rings calling everybody to samu (work, primarily physical, performed with attention and seriousness but by no means solemnity), go out and confer with person in charge of cleaning about what needs to be done to which rooms and when. Return to godo's room, make bed, remove morning tea and wash, empty ashtrays in small sitting room now empty. Someone comes to door, a lost-looking, diffident and inarticulate young German who can't find his zafu and wants to buy material to sew himself a rakusu. Commiserate over zafu, insisting that in the end they turn up and are never lost (but with his looks and obvious ill luck, maybe they are sometimes) and lead him up two flights to sewing-room on top floor, where fifteen men and women are stitching away by hand and on machines in an atmosphere of concentration, haste and relaxed chatter. A favorite place, littered every night with scraps and threads and dirty dishes and clutter, out of which emerge the beautiful things we wear. Japanese things, or from the Indo-Chinese-Japanese tradition. Not culturally ours, difficult to sew—but thus far, impossible to improve upon. They've been perfecting them for so many hundreds of years. Except for the rakusus and kesas: we use the traditional designs, down to the last half centimeter; but on the whole we sew them more beautifully and painstakingly than the Japanese nowadays, perhaps because they are fresh and foreign to us, but certainly because our master felt so deeply about them and taught us so intently.

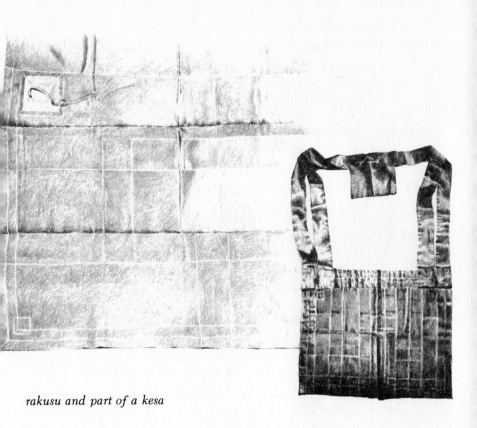

rakusu and part of a kesa

ONE AFTERNOON BEFORE
the chemotherapy began I had
to wait around upstairs in the
ward for some tests, and was sitting smoking in the hall with a
couple of inpatients and a nurse
rolling bandages. She said, The
wonderful thing about this place
is that you don't have to think
for yourself, they do it all for
you.

I goggled, but said nothing: there were other people around who seemed to concur with her and meddling in people's self-comfort is a tricky business, not to be engaged in lightly.

There was also Frieda.

I think I first talked to Frieda waiting to be tested by the ear doctor. I had seen her before maybe twice, once in the place we all went, if we could walk, to get a drop of blood taken from a fingertip every morning, and again in a hall, in the chemotherapy ward or the electrocardiogram unit or somewhere. She was sixty and a bit, good strong white wavy hair, very small, no more than five feet, a shade plump but firm, big, forthright dark brown eyes and straight eyebrows and a broad straight forehead and a profile so clean as almost to qualify as patrician, but tough, strong, cal-loused hands and broad small stumpy feet. She sat and stood very straight too, but there was a lot of weight on her shoulders. She had a thick Alsatian accent but made almost no mistakes in French, which is unusual here. She was clear and intelligent. She was a rarity, a true peasant. She lived in a village fifteen miles or so south of town, with her mother who was eighty-six or eighty-eight.

We discovered that we were preparing for the same chemo-therapy and were scheduled to begin the same day. She had had an operation a few months back but didn't know what exactly had been done to her. She also didn't know exactly what she was there for now. She was doing what the doctor told her. She did not like knowing so little and was resentful on that point, but she had not the habit of demanding explanations and she certainly had a distaste for long words. She did not like the idea of this clinic, which was named after some man without any reference to cancer or any other disease but which was known to many people in town and around as a place you only came out of feet first. She hadn't told her mother where she went on the mornings when she came to town. She could take taxis and get the money back afterwards but it meant filling out forms and was complicated. I offered to drive her in the next time she had to come. She accepted. She invited me to visit that Sunday afternoon. It was difficult to arrange because she had no telephone but there was a neighbor one could call.

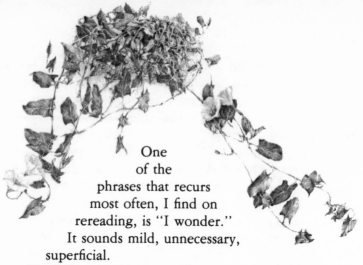

One
of the
phrases that recurs
most often, I find on
rereading, is "I wonder."
It sounds mild, unnecessary,
superficial.

Kodo Sawaki, Sensei's master, wrote somewhere that whatever success he had had in his career with disciples could be attributed to his conviction, his absolute certainty.

I agree: nothing convinces like conviction. But we are all seeing so much damage done by conviction nowadays. . . . Many people who would like nothing better than to be convinced, in a positive direction, automatically reject anything that sounds categorical and prefer to go on suffering from indefiniteness. Even if that means they can never see anything straight and live and die muddled.

In part their hesitation is justified, moreover, insofar as it comes from a suspicion that there is more than one side to it, whatever it is.

Wondering, as I mean it, is constant, mild in the sense that the prodding to light a cigarette is mild for a confirmed smoker surrounded by equipment but not mild at all if there are no cigarettes at hand or nothing to light them with and all the stores are closed, or there is some strong legal or moral inhibition at work to prevent the lighting of the cigarette.

Then the prodding becomes steely, it can lead to a low moan and eventually a shriek. That's the kind of wondering I mean.

Superficial it may be, as the smoker's addiction is superficial—although the smoker doesn't know that. To the smoker it is gut-deep.

Wondering, like curiosity, is akin to fear. Fortunately, we have them because we would never have got off all fours otherwise; but for real progress they need to be tempered by other forces. So often fear gets out of hand, as in our longing to have things settled "one way or the other," which leads straight to destruction. Or to computers. On–off. Yes–no.

Destruction is so simple. It relieves the strain. I sometimes think we have devised entropy to justify destruction. "That's the nature of the universe."

There's no need for the strain. That's not the only nature of the universe.

During the sesshin last week at La Gendronnière godo talked at some length about the error of wanting to do away with one's illusions, trying to "get better," wanting to be free of ego-trips and -trammels. Can't be done, he said; mustn't be tried.

True. But every day, once or twice, we chant BONNO MUJIN SEIGANDAN, which means, roughly, "However innumerable passions-attachments-illusions may be, I vow to put an end to them."

That's where it's at: neither the one nor the other, and not (in any mathematical sense) both. In the tension, in the ground where nothing is known and there is no certainty, there is the way.

For some years I have thought that two American college songs were close to it, and have chortled them in my head meditating or driving along the roads, with a smug idea that as long as they were being bawled out on the campuses the system, all the systems, could not, however hard they tried, entirely demolish the youth of my native land.

One is:

Oh, the bear went over the mountain,
The bear went over the mountain,
The bear went over the mountain
To see what he could see.

The other side of the mountain,
The other side of the mountain,
The other side of the mountain
Was all that he could see.

IT WAS HALLOWE'EN IN New Orleans. I explained as well as I could what that meant, and Sensei wanted to see. We walked the streets taking pictures of every conceivable sort of costume and nakedness. Dressed as always in his monk's garb, he wanted his picture taken with some of them: one amazing pair of breasts, a Dracula or so, a couple of girls got up as nuns on whose cheeks he planted a kiss; and in every case there was a tiny gleam of puzzlement.

Finally, somebody put it into words: "Is he real?"

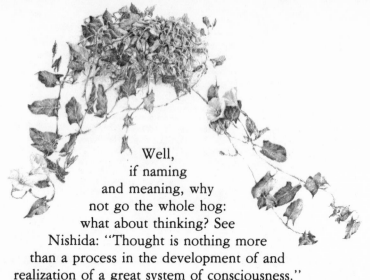

Well,
if naming
and meaning, why
not go the whole hog:
what about thinking? See
Nishida: "Thought is nothing more
than a process in the development of and
realization of a great system of consciousness."
Just one process, intermediate.

Which brings us to the gates of the Big Bang and the physics of subatomic particles.

One way of sizing up, sizing down rather, the ego. Another is sitting at a table in the dining room during sesshin while the food is being dealt out. One dish or platter for six, one person distributes to five others and him or herself. More or less openly, almost if not absolutely everyone has calculated the size of the portions before the distributor's spoon or knife descends, and knows whether he or she is getting a fair share. The distributor may dish out once without regard to what's left for himself or herself, but not twice. It complicates matters, too, because then other people have to give some back, creating debts and awarenesses of stinginess or aggressive liberality.

Do not look one side only, said Sensei. Being conscious, without thinking, of everything, will enable you to hand out the food precisely and have enough left for yourself. The result will be simple and exact, and so will the process; as with the subatomic particles, which would appear to be "simple" and exact and very possibly conscious, although almost certainly not thinking.

DOWN HALL TO ROOM, RE-move cardigan and wool T-shirt, stare out window at copper beech outside and people pushing wheelbarrows of earth fill for grass on the far side of the tomb mound and digging weeds out of courtyard gravel; if you lean out you can see others at tables behind the kitchen chopping vegetables in the sun, and children playing around the "sauna" house.

Sit on bed facing typewriter on chair, open English translation of Dogen text and begin rattling it into rudimentary French. Pause, eat a cookie. Type. Pause, light a cigarette, type.

At noon, bonsho rings the end of samu. People go to shower, put tools away, sit in sun or under trees with books.

Take translation to godo who's not there, collect white kimono, now dry but still smelling of fish, go to office in search of auditor who is the kind of man who might possess a scent that could camouflage the mackerel, give in chits for purchases and get reimbursed, except for cigarettes ordered by people who often can't pay for them or try not to—a situation that can become highly irritating and tricky, demanding patience, tact and cunning. Collect list of people for ordination and folder containing their letters, photos, life histories, pass through big drawing room and note remains of impromptu meeting at table. Godo is back, discuss text of translation and problem of mackerel, search out story about Fuke and the seamless garment (i.e., coffin) he wanted, clean up big drawing room and prepare table to serve coffee for heads-of-dojo meeting after lunch.

The metal clangs. The bell-girl is there ready, no godo. Put on kesa and wait. No use looking for him, he'll find himself. He arrives, throws on robe and kesa. Go to lunch. Sutra. On the wall behind godo and other officials is a large photograph of Sensei grinning. Sometimes, grin back at it. Food, comments thereon. Some people find that carrots come too often and meat not often enough, others the reverse. Announcements.

WE HAD THREE HOURS in Atlanta. Get a taxi, he said, we shall look at the city. I got a taxi, driven by an uncommunicative Black with a sax on the seat beside him. He was not interested in expatiating on the parts of town, what was new, what was special about Atlanta. But in the end he loosened a bit.

Suddenly Sensei was hungry; where could we eat at an hour when nobody ate in restaurants, and close enough to the airport to have some chance of not missing the next plane? The driver worked over it awhile and finally came up with a place. He would wait outside in the car and play his sax, he said; I told him that if we weren't out by a certain time he was to come in and get us. He said, Yeah.

While we were there Sensei wanted to use the toilet. He left and returned a few minutes later waving a key attached to a long stick. "Why keep toilet locked?" he asked. I said, To keep out the Blacks. His secretary gasped at what she identified as my paranoia or racism and immediately claimed it couldn't be true. I said, We'll ask, and called over the woman who ran the place. "This Japanese gentleman wants to know why the toilet door has to be locked," I said. And she answered, "To keep out strays." Strays, I said, means Blacks. His secretary looked dismayed and disgusted.

Sensei said to her, severely, "You must understand karma of this country, karma of South, karma of Negroes. Not simple." Realizing that the driver would not come in after us, I got us out in time.

The
thing is
that the morning
after Sensei's death
was telephoned to us in
Paris, I took that train down to
Blois to see the doctor who was supposed
to prescribe a diet for me during chemotherapy and
forever after.

It was the last day of April and the flat fields of Beauce were green. It was a particularly Aprilish day, with an affable pale-blue sky and clouds here and there and some rain in places. I stared out the window and considered how I felt, which was on the whole ordinary. Perhaps a little lighter than sometimes; perhaps a little more diffuse, less hard-edged. The strips of spring color unrolled, willows by stream-banks, old stone farms; crept into the corners of my sight and brain, soaked through my whole head. I looked up at the affable pale sky and clouds and thought, There is nothing missing in the whole universe. He gave us everything we need. The work was done.

I had seldom felt so calmly in harmony with things. The moment did not seem significant at the time but it has become so since. But its significance doesn't come out the way statements announced as having significance usually do.

No; the direct continuation of that thought, which I have just had now, almost two years later, is: And since then I don't know what I am doing.

Also an affable feeling, if somewhat light-headed.

JEAN AND I DROVE OUT TO
Frieda's village. The little farmhouse was dwarfed by more imposing ones behind, beside and
across from it. No modern con-
veniences except electricity and
running water, cold. A little
dog, quite a few plants in pots,
of sorts I hadn't seen before,
great-granddaughters of plants
now out of fashion; strawberries and raspberry canes, rhubarb,
currant bushes, gooseberries, cabbages and lettuces and carrots and
onions, a tiny orchard with apples and plums and mirabelles and
plants that were good for burns and plants that were good for
constipation and plants that made the blood stop running if you cut
yourself; and some laying hens and a good thirty ducks and duck-
lings that were a problem and worried her because they made so
much work for her mother when she had to be away. Outside the
village there were about twenty-five acres, in hay and beetroot—
one time they had planted tobacco but she was sure it had made
them all sick—and nine cows, but those lived at her brother's, who
was also unmarried; he had another little farmhouse in the same
village. If she had to be away a long time her other brother, who
had been a postman and was retired, would have to be called in to
help. He wasn't much good, I gathered, but would be better than
nothing. She sold ducks' eggs and milk and churned her own butter
and sold that to people in the village, and made the little bit of cash
they needed to buy fuel for the tractor and the young pig they
fattened each year and killed for ham that she cured herself.

We had tea in the parlor with the old lady; the brother came
in and ate what was probably his main meal while we were there,
cutting slices from a ham the hide of which was a shiny ebony crust.
The old mother wore heavy wool stockings in June and served us

a very sweet wine she made; but she had little time for such foreigners. There were photographs on the wall of long ago; Frieda regarded them with no affection and volunteered no information about them. I later learned she had had a fiancé, I believe he was killed in the early days of the Second World War.

We duly turned up on the morning we were scheduled to begin the chemotherapy. She had asked a few questions at other moments and I had answered to the best of my ability but without flatly affirming things, staying in the realm of "Some people think that . . ." and "Sometimes it can happen that . . ." Shortly after lunch the nurses wheeled in their equipment and prepared to hook us up. Frieda was in the bed opposite and there were two other women in the room. She said to the nurse bearing down on her, Will that thing make my hair fall out, and the nurse rolled about a bit but finally said, It's pretty likely to, whereupon Frieda said, Then I don't want it. Tell the doctor I want to see him.

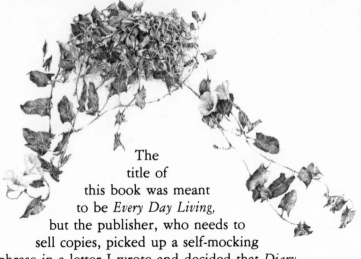

The
title of
this book was meant
to be *Every Day Living,*
but the publisher, who needs to
sell copies, picked up a self-mocking
phrase in a letter I wrote and decided that *Diary
of a Zen Nun* it would have to be. I protested vehemently but to
no avail—well, that's my problem. But if you don't mind, we'll go
on as if it was still called *Every Day Living.*

The point of Every Day Living, as a title: what does Zen look
like realized?

In me, this assumes the hortatory tones of a classroom demonstration. Now, children, have you all got the point? Thirty years ago
at college Professor Barbara Swain cautioned, "You'll need to look
out for dogmatism, my dear." Thirty years of uneasy observation
later, I conclude that you can't fight city hall; whence the aforementioned aspect, as built into me as into Walt Whitman and (underneath the art) Saul Bellow. It is an embarrassment to be borne, like
a habit of farting in public.

Moreover, what Zen looks like realized can only be: nothing
special; so it's a hopeless contradiction.

But the masters have also been writing for two thousand years
as though it were something special.

One of my favorite "ways in" is the old story that shows the
essence of the master-discipline relationship.

The master and his disciple were attending a funeral, the disciple pointed to the corpse and asked, "Is that dead or alive?" The

master answered, "I cannot say." The disciple threatened to strike the master, who said, "You can hit me all you like, but I cannot say whether that is dead or alive."

So the disciple struck him. That evening the master told the others what had happened and announced that the disciple would have to leave because he had struck the master.

So the disciple went off to another master and told his tale, hoping to hear that the first master was a cruel monster and off his nut. Instead of which, the second master exclaimed, "What a compassionate master you had there!" Whereupon the disciple began to see what it was all about.

It is not the tricky answer that counts, it is what the disciple does with it.

Forging the metaphor. Like putting the bridle together, forging the metaphor is composed of observable acts, but it *is* not observable acts.

RUN BACK TO SMALL kitchen, take coffee down to big drawing room and begin to serve. Check that somebody is taking notes. Speak once, to suggest that other people need to be heard from (there is a terrible tendency among those who teach never to let go of the floor once they've got it) and another time to try to pin down a decision which seemed to have been made but not carried through and which will otherwise, as so often, sink away into the sands. It is very difficult to hold any of these people to an intention because they have learned to shift with the moment, act in the here-now, and know that what they might plan to do six months (six minutes) from now won't happen the way they plan it anyway. But for insecure hesitant people running a zazen group of six or seven souls somewhere in the sticks, plans and earnests of support are necessary.

Extra-
ordinary;
it's taken them
six days to travel
eighty miles. Last Thursday
morning, driving north from Basel
along the Rhine, I saw the swifts, rambling
thousands, tumbling and scooping northward in a
thready, hesitant, irresistible front. For ten miles I ran alongside
them, then lost them as the road turned away from the river. At
lunch that day I announced that summer was on its way and would
surely reach Strasbourg that night or the next morning, but waited
in vain.

Now, the following Wednesday morning, from a temporary
office at the top of the parliament building, suddenly I see them,
here they come, just arriving. Most seem to be heading generally
northward so perhaps these too will pass through and the Strasbourg swifts are still on the road. It never occurred to me they
would travel so slowly, once they got within striking distance of
their nesting towns.

Everything has been late. Winter did not begin until February
25. February 25 was the pits. The snow and cold came then, when
plants were already gathering themselves to grow. March 10 was
suddenly heaven. Then more muddle. Then just before Palm Sunday, midsummer weather, and everything started to blossom at
once. The magnolias were out and gone in four days. My garden
was all mixed up, arabis and iberis and aubrietia and tulips and
daffodils and bleeding-hearts and forget-me-nots and lilies of the

valley and primroses and scilla and grape hyacinths and snowdrops and phlox subulata virtually all at once, and now a short panting pause while the iris and peonies swell (they're late, like the chestnuts): only gillyflowers to be seen and aquilegia starting and coral bells.

The larks rose late. The blackbirds sang late. My eyes were late. And then there was a dry spell with all that warmth, so that leaves on the forest trees opened but everything at ground level remained parched, and then suddenly the nightingales arrived early and there was nowhere for them to hide, so for about a week one saw them quite often fluttering about in the old brown leaves. There are fewer this year, some of their stations are still vacant. Fewer swallows too. Where were the losses heavy, over the sea or in Italian nets or African droughts or what? The trees where the orioles have nested for years have been cut down but I heard one not too far away. The ratio of cuckoos remains unchanged, only one for quite a large patch of woodland in these parts; I have almost never heard more than one calling at the same time.

Our affairs in the sangha change and remain the same. Zazen every morning in town among six or eight or fifteen of us is one easy and terribly difficult thing; zazen in sesshin at La Gendronnière or (less) elsewhere is another terribly difficult and easy thing. Town is easy on the ego and hard on the effort, sesshin is tough on the ego and easy on effort. If such a distinction can be in any sense meaningful.

FROM ASHEVILLE TO CHARLOTTESVILLE the drive was longer than I figured (speed limits are so much higher in Europe), but the roads were empty: it was election day. Sensei said he had watched a television debate a few nights before in Chicago and was clear that Reagan would win: "He stronger." The next morning we drove from Charlottesville to Washington, and Reagan had won.

The capital was absolutely empty; a great day for visiting it. He wanted lunch but I didn't dare leave a hired car illegally parked in the nation's capital so I sat outside while the others ate. Having found time to visit yet another souvenir shop he reappeared, and presented me with a Reagan button, knowing that was not my choice. I growled, "But I don't *like* Reagan," and he said, "Not important. Reagan President."

It became true with those words. His style—"not necessary too much diplomatic"—taught us what our own teachers had been unable to: that by *not quite* accepting, because they do not please us, things that are so, we spend our entire lives making meaningless gestures somewhere next door to reality.

Sure, life is a dream: it *really* is a dream. And not a fuzzy dream.

THE FIRST PRODUCT DID
not have much effect that I could
feel, so I was still ready to talk
afterwards. Frieda had said at
one point that she was a Protestant and I had seen that there
was a multi-denominational
chapel downstairs at the clinic
and that the Protestant service
would be held that evening. I

told her. She said she was worried about what her mother would
think or do if she, Frieda, lost her hair. She needed to consult
somebody. In the end she asked me to help her telephone to the
neighbor who would fetch someone she could talk to—I thought
she said her mother but that seemed odd if she didn't want her to
know. We went down to the telephone and I showed her the
chapel.

Then I went back upstairs and made a zafu out of a blanket and
pillows and sat in zazen on the floor next to the bed. When she came
in I was still sitting. She got into bed and said nothing. When I was
back in bed too she said, Was that like praying, what you were
doing, and I said, Yes, pretty much. She said, I thought so. After
a little while, she began to sing a Protestant hymn aloud in a high,
clear voice. The next morning she went down to see the head of
chemotherapy and came back a little grim but on the whole pleased
with herself. He had been fairly bullying and told her she had one
chance in a hundred to make it on her own. She had said, One
chance in a hundred? I'll take it, and come away again. She had a
book about honey and vinegar and intended to buy some plants at
the herb shop in town, and she would go home and see what
happened. Yes, she would see a doctor. Maybe we could give her
the name of a homeopathic one.

She stayed all that day and left the next afternoon, just as I was getting into my stride in the first bout of every-ten-minutes-like-clockwork heaving and retching. She looked at me with what might have been impatience or a little disgust as she went out the door and said something like, Good luck, you'll need it.

We went back to the village a month later, and Frieda was swinging down the street on her bicycle. Her local doctor had told her to get rid of her few extra pounds and cut down on the cheese and milk. She was tired, though, and she said so.

Frieda has not got very much to do with what troubles me in all this. She would know what she had to do whatever the circumstances. Doctors and nurses and patients lost definition, became blurred and pale when they were around her, although she was certainly anything but overbearing.

I haven't been back since, I don't know what happened to Frieda. I don't want her to be dead or dying.

Coming
back to work
on mornings after
riding, when I have
seen such beautiful things—
one day recently there were five
deer in different parts of the forest, quite
unafraid, and lots of hares—and there is most
wonderful music on the car radio or fascinating programs about the
latest state of the Big Bang theory. . . .

"When people first hear about the Big Bang theory they imagine a sort of extremely hard rock in an emptiness that suddenly explodes [all those words assuming a where and a when!]. But Einstein showed that space-time-and-matter could not be separated. Which means that the Big Bang [which "happened"?] didn't produce only matter, it also gave birth to space and time. There was nothing 'before' [but what if the Big Bang by which our scholars are preoccupied was only one of an unlimited series of Big Bangs followed by little whimpers, and our notions of "before" and "after" need still further amplification?], not even empty space, there wasn't any 'outside' into which any Big Bang could have exploded." (And yet, it apparently did.)

A Sunday morning in Paris twenty years ago, Easter Sunday, just back from Ischia followed by Portofino; I lay coiled, a reptilian having overfed, in the apartment of a dead friend on the Rue de Vaugirard at the back of a courtyard, ground floor, dirt cheap, improvised bathroom, littered with precious books and bibelots from all over the world, tiny, cramped, dusty, now awaiting definitive disposal, and I awaiting a definitive interview; I put on a record of Benjamin Britten's *War Requiem* and lay there with the blinds drawn in the empty apartment that nobody lived in or loved anymore, so dusty, so much the nest of a bird that meant to stay only a season and was still there twenty years later being crowded out by all the glittering trinkets it had amassed, but now just a husk of nest; listening in the sunny spring morning while the whole of Paris was at church and me only lurking behind shutters; and so lightly, loosely, so completely unbidden, at no particular note or moment, I sensed a turning-on, saw a gesture—a hand fully formed where no hand had been, switching on a switch: "on"—and never again, from that day, did I totally reject religious belief. The hand I attributed to an imagination impoverished by calendar art in infancy, and dismissed; but the nothing and then "after" (no before, but an after), that I kept. Along with the tiny breach in the buckler of my woolly pseudo-Marxist cynicism.

. . . I wonder what happens to all the riches and splendor I have absorbed. Because some old puritanical need to justify delight makes me want the birds and beasts and flowers and clouds and smells and harmonies to rub off, to do somebody some good.

Keizan (thirteenth century) says, however, Make yourself into a censer in which there is not one trace of incense.

If you must create karma at least let it be good karma; but since one man's good is another man's poison the best thing is to create none at all.

But about the only time you create none at all, or close to it, is in zazen.

Which leaves us where we were before. (This thought process, I mean: zazen does not leave us where we were before.)

AT 2:30 BONSHO RINGS again for samu but the meeting isn't over. Nail a girl to do the washing-up at the end of it and leave, to confer about ordinations and the state of sewing and the calligrapher's mood. One monk-to-be has handed a kesa in to the office without saying who sewed it; in several other cases, the people handing in kesas and rakusus for calligraphy before ordination have put the civilian name but not the religious name of the person or persons doing the sewing, so that means get out the files and, where they are complete, copy out the religious name and meaning; where they are not, find the sewer and ask, or get his or her rakusu and make a photocopy of it.

Find out where the monk-to-be sleeps by consulting the chart on the reception desk (it has disappeared under people folding and stuffing envelopes; search and search in mounting perplexity and ill-temper; and find). In one of the tents, third bed from the end. Go to the tent—third bed from which end? There should be nobody in the tent; everybody should be working; there are two people in it. One is in bed and doesn't know which bed belongs to the monk-to-be, the other is the mournful German of this morning who also doesn't know which bed belongs to the monk-to-be but who proffers, with embarrassed courtliness, a cheap Japanese fan, saying, "You first lady come into this tent. Here—for zazen posture —next year." This enigma will be unraveled later, no doubt, in conversation with other Germans who are deeper into the intricacies of this one's mind. In the meantime the monk-to-be is not to be found. Abandon, on to the next, a nun-to-be.

She turns out to live upstairs in the former stables but is predictably not there; bump into her by chance on the way back from the stables. "Oh, ever so many people sewed on my kesa, I don't even know all their names." Okay, that means the calligrapher writes "Sewed by the sangha" on it.

HE WANTED TO SEE Philadelphia; I didn't. We got there after nightfall and spent a quarter of an hour being impressed by the town's center and amazed by the suddenness of the division between white and black, rich and poor. We got lost trying to find our way out of town back to the expressway. Sensei's secretary was in the back seat with the map, navigating; Sensei was asleep in front.

I found an expressway of sorts and started north on it; she told me it ended in a field. Nonsense, I said; I can't believe any American expressway ends in a field, all of them are connected, eventually this will lead us over to the Jersey pike. For once I overrode her, on the grounds that I had to know better about the roads of my own country.

It ended in a field. I grabbed the map, figured out some kind of course that involved going backwards over side roads, and drove on. Sensei was cross because driving bored him; his secretary was cross because I had disobeyed and was wasting time, and I was very cross because I hadn't wanted to go to Philadelphia and had probably disregarded her directions on that account. However, as the flak started to come down I was helped by the presence of the steering wheel and said, I guess the most important thing is that I should keep us on the road and not in the trees, and everybody shut up again.

Half an hour or so later, out of the corner of one eye I saw the Jersey Turnpike sign with an arrow flash past and began to breathe. But then we were suddenly on a big expressway heading for Baltimore. Sensei's secretary snapped and scolded, and he woke up and said, in a big deep voice, "Driver no good, we go backwards." Whereupon his secretary climbed another note up the scale.

But it was such a big deep voice that I sneaked a look at him and saw he was grinning: he had also seen, and recognized (although how I can't imagine), the Jersey pike sign and knew we were all right.

Now,
this very
day, has come
another of those
trying moments.
This morning we found some twenty
wasps buzzing weakly against the living room curtains or
dead or dying on the floor. As the windows were both shut, one
couldn't imagine where they had come from. I went to work thinking that at least they would keep the cat amused and possibly deter
him from his usual round of picture-smashing and plant-upsetting
and carpet-shredding. At noon they were still there, more numerous than before.

Above the window is an overhang, papered and painted and,
I had always assumed, encasing some solid beam that supported the
roof. In the extreme corner of this overhang was a dark spot a little
more than half an inch across. Splash of paint? No black paint in
the room. No; a hole. And above it, somewhere in the inexplicable
entrails of the roof structure, a wasps' nest. How had they ever
gotten in? If that space was not sealed on the outside, we should
have had rainwater cascading down the walls. Also, I did not know
that wasps ate through plaster and paint and, presumably at some
point, wood.

Was one, on the principle of nonintervention in the cosmic
order, to let them establish themselves permanently? One thing
sure, they would scare the cleaning lady so that she would never
go into the room again. I got out the vacuum and removed those
that offered no resistance.

I went up to the attic and looked around—no wasps. I brought down the tall ladder—to inspect was my only intention at that point. I climbed up and inspected—just as another full-bodied, lacquered, bright new wasp was unfolding itself through the hole. I climbed down, again with no conscious intention but remembering where I had seen something the same color of gray as the wall, went to the sewing drawer, took out a leather elbow patch that matched the paint almost perfectly, scissors, and a tube of glue. I climbed back up, wasps weaving alertly around me, and glued them in.

Is that how all murders are committed? At no moment in this process of unconscious escalation did I think what I was about to do.

Detachment. I do not feel at all pleased with myself, and on the other hand I am almost sure the wasps will have chewed their way through the leather in very short order and other steps will have to be taken. And now the wasp-smotherer returns to the office.

LOOK FOR THE CALLIGRA-pher, in a room upstairs over the kitchen. He's not there but his five-year-old daughter is asleep on the bed. Down the hall to the barman's room to ask him to bring up a case of beer and put it in godo's refrigerator in the cellar. Discuss briefly the success and failure of measures to control the few hard-core drinkers who have not yet made their way out of the pre–Sensei's-death period; and the psychological, academic and other aspects of the barman's teen-age sons.

Up to the next floor to leave some money in the empty room of the monk who sells salt-pickled plums, in payment for a bag for godo who likes them in his morning tea. Down that hall to the photographer's room to see what film people are watching on the video. They all ought to be working but there's almost always a small crowd, the older children and a few lazy adults, half-asleep in midafternoon, lolling in a haze of smoke and groggy with airless-ness. It's a spy story about a triple agent. Sit for a few minutes with an arm around the neck of a totally unconscious alcoholic friend: all energy, one hopes and trusts, goes somewhere.

Back to the sewing-room to check a few more kesas and raku-sus. Bring lists up to date and check with those in office. Bonsho rings 4 P.M., end of samu.

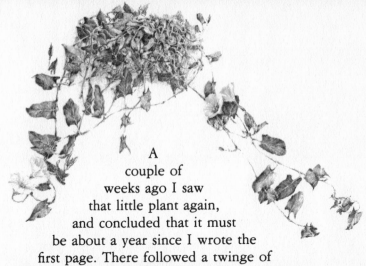

A
couple of
weeks ago I saw
that little plant again,
and concluded that it must
be about a year since I wrote the
first page. There followed a twinge of
dismay, because I couldn't remember its name!

So what is one pretending to do? So it isn't possible to learn anything when one reaches my advanced age? Confirmation, at any rate, of the fact that you only know what you use.

In the ensuing day or two the name did come back to me, lesser bindweed. But with doubts, because this plant, as I saw it then among the cornfields and on the paths, did not look very bindy at all. Spreading and sprawly but not binding.

Last night I checked, and the name was right. So it is possible to learn things at my advanced age, even if one does not use them regularly.

I also wish to report that the lesser bindweed does indeed bind when it can get hold of anything to wrap itself round, that it is more in evidence this year than last, there is in fact quite a lot of it, good thick mats. It is very healthy this year and full of flowers. The original question, Is it a pest to farmers?, arises again.

Whose relationship with the lesser bindweed am I worried about?

What with summer being so late, the cherries are only now ripe on the trees. In my sampling rides these mornings, I have spied several more vine-peach trees and am carefully monitoring their

progress. The fact that there are quite a few of them is gladdening because it means more peaches to eat; but it also means more chances that somebody else knows and cares about them and will harvest the crop, and not take kindly to it being surreptitiously removed by a presumably idle and monied woman on horseback.

The lapwings may be increasing in numbers; or changing locale. Six of them have taken up residence on the low swells of fields where I sample cherries, and as I come through they fly up and circle round and round, irregularly and at some distance, but keeping me well covered until I am out of their territory. Only one cries at a time. I am not sure whether these are this year's young or molting parents; certainly they do not have crests, and there are occasional feathers missing in wings and tail. The other day as I cantered up a long rise one of them swung alongside, maybe fifteen feet away, and kept just level with us as we came on. I cannot decide whether they are being companionable or trying to mob me.

A day or so ago while I was in their territory I heard a sharp scolding birdcry somewhere else and looked around to identify it. Across the road a small bird of prey, kestrel or sparrow hawk, was trying to chase a buzzard. I rode toward them and one or two of the lapwings came with me, although it was outside their usual flying ground. When they saw what was up, all the lapwings joined in and drove off the buzzard, while the smaller hawk disappeared.

I always wonder why buzzards let themselves be so easily intimidated. A real mob I could understand, but one or two lapwings it could easily catch, I should think. Perhaps it wasn't really hunting and is just a sort of compulsive marauding bully.

We must be careful in extrapolating from animal behavior. They simply harmonize with what happens, they can make no conscious effort to change their karma; it changes when evolution, in one form or another, makes it change.

We on the other hand can change our karma, although only when it becomes conscious. We may not have the built-in mechanisms of the animals that prevent them from destroying their own species; but we are free in a way they are not.

Harmonizing is more of a problem for us. Better than a problem, it's a beautiful springboard: which do you harmonize with? Which is the cosmic order? Your cancer or your cure?

IN THE MOTEL IN New Jersey he picked up a Japanese in the elevator, who stuck to us the whole last day. That was Bronx Zoo day. It was November and a lot of things were shut but there was still plenty to look at, and for Sensei the Bronx Zoo was as important as Niagara. In the gorilla house he stopped dead: various large apes were doing various things behind the glass, but there was one old codger sitting at the front, very much in the posture of Rodin's *Thinker.*

"Ha!" said Sensei. "I teach zazen posture, right posture, to Western people, they all sit falling over like Rodin sculpture, only use forebrain, only think dualism, cannot create, and look, Western gorilla do same thing!"

THAT WAS ONE OF THE tricks one had to learn: how to be with the other patients. Some of them didn't know they had cancer and didn't want to know. Some knew and were giving up. Some knew and pretended not to. There were no private rooms —that was an odd moment, when the head of chemotherapy  announced to me that there were no private rooms almost with a glimmer of hope, as though he was sure I would mind, that would be part of my general orneriness and might even make me go away; but I said it didn't matter in the slightest—and so I found myself with an assortment of women, different every month, and we all had to make some sort of space for one another in our heads.

It was fairly hard work. I was always comparing them, who is sicker than whom, they are sicker than I, let me never be as sick as they are, and separating myself from them; but there was the other movement too, please don't be so sick, I ought to be as sick as you are so you can feel better, I ought to be sicker than you, and joining myself to them. Mostly they did not want to make conversation.

The place itself was middling horrible. Only walls to see outside the windows, a lot of heat.

The treatment was not horrible at all, because the buffer state was in full sway. I have spoken about it once or twice since then and felt half-faint myself at one point; but then and there it was just what was happening. I read Boswell, or pretended to, while hanging around waiting for X-rays and lymphangiograms; I read Géroudet's books on songbirds, slowly, carefully and without retaining a word of them, while the various chemicals were going in and out of my veins. I corrected proofs when I had them. Benjamin brought meals at noon and sometimes he and Jean stayed to eat with me, but that was only the first two days each time. In the middle of the second night the night-duty nurse came to hook me up to the hydrating drip and after that I did no more eating until the nausea wore off four days later.

The third day was rough, of course; they put the platinum through at nine in the morning and exactly three hours later I began to be sick and continued without intermission for six to eight hours. It turned out to be a useful experience later, irrefutable proof of the nonexistence of a permanent unchanging self: when one is surrounded by bowls and basins containing everything one has voided, one way or another, over a period of eighteen hours, because it must all be measured and what comes out must be exactly equal to what goes in, one is so literally an exploded body, a bunch of mutant fragments.

Last
night we
went to dinner
to meet a couple of
wonderful old men who
have apparently lived together
as bachelors forever; they began
collecting medieval statues and pottery
before the war, fled to Algiers when Alsace was
retaken by the Germans and returned after the war to find their
collections gone, turned to seventeenth- and eighteenth-century
Italian and French painting instead and have now, their hometown
having declined to shelter or otherwise accommodate their collection as often seems to be the case, given it to the Louvre where it
is on display.

They travel about in their Mercedes to hear operas in Salzburg
or attend sales in London, one of them does the shopping and the
other one cooks and, I think probably, pinches pennies; the one
who shops mumbles a little and seems slightly gaga until you ask
him about the opera they heard in Munich last week when he drily
comments "Mediocre," while the one who cooks has a game leg
or perhaps an artificial one and slaving over a hot stove would seem
to be out of the question for him. They are what one would have
to call "old dears," and a great deal more.

I would not care to offer an opinion on some bit of Glück or
Handel in their presence unless I was prepared to face a firing squad
over it. Not that they would say anything, being old dears. But the
drafty vastness of my ignorance would sweep through the room like

a gale while one of them stared bleakly at his shoetip and the other sipped mint tea.

I held forth at the dinner table on the habits of lapwings and peasant farmers in the bit of north central Alsace I ride through and at one point mentioned a cherry tree I had found that very morning that bore black cherries on one half of it and white cherries on the other. "Graft," said one of the old dears. Yes, but so long ago that the old tree has assumed an entirely natural aspect and its bicolored fruits are quite startling.

I said I would pick some so they could see. So this morning I set off with a plastic bowl tied up in a scarf and a halter with which to attach Golden Gate to a tree for the few short minutes it would take to pick cherries. I haven't tried tying him to a tree or anything other than a ring in the stable for four or five years, but I should have known better. In his case, age is irrelevant. As I was deftly wrapping the halter rope around a branch he gave one good backward pull, slipped down the bank, and that was that.

It is interesting to watch the process of his realizing that he is free. It takes about two seconds, I think, one can almost see his pea-brain registering "no contact" as he checks up and down his body; the information pours into his neurons, his head lifts, he takes two exploratory strides at an airy trot, and *whoosh.*

On this occasion he was cheered on gleefully by a family of farmers who had just trundled past on their tractor. I watched him settle, after a few hundred yards of inefficient wild plunging, into a strong, erect, businesslike working gallop for the stable, swore at him and decided I was not going to wring my hands over him as on previous occasions.

I turned my back before he was out of sight and started picking cherries, although I did wonder a few seconds later whether the cherries would be equal to the situation if he came a cropper before he reached his box or caused a major road accident. It seemed to me at the time that almost nothing could shake the extreme good humor of the morning.

The cherries got picked, the rider walked back, the horse was waiting, still all harnessed but shut into his box, wearing it seemed to me a rather concentrated, fierce expression, as, "What's she going to try this time?" I made puny threats, mounted and rode him dry. As always, he was almost docile after his stunt.

Hélène made the cherries into a *clafouti* and it got delivered to the friends who invited us to dinner last night.

I find such things highly satisfying: some object, cherries or leaves, gets picked by one person and cooked or painted on by somebody else and given on some significant (highly or feebly) pretext to somebody else. I like the manyness and mixture, the work and care, the ceremony, the all-inclusiveness of the process, object and thought and energy and skill and persons all brought together.

Tonight, on the other hand, I rather dread. It is my turn to be godo for the week here in the Strasbourg dojo, and I have decided to talk about something called the Go-I and so variously translated that it's not worth trying, but which is reputed to be central to Soto Zen. It is related by some people to dialectics, but I am less and less sure that the comparison is useful.

It may have to do with the way in which absolute and relative stand to each other; but as I think about it I do not see that it is possible to say, in words—or any other way for that matter—anything about the absolute. Yet for thousands of years wiser people than I have been doing it. Our own master talked about the Go-I for weeks and then suddenly stopped, maybe because some of the disciples said, "Please, Sensei, we don't understand a syllable of all that, teach us something else."

I don't know what use it is, I don't know why we have to do it. But it is very clear to me that we have to. Indians took Buddhism to China and the Chinese spent centuries translating and worrying over and transforming the texts before they could start creating their own—one of the first of which was this ridiculous Go-I. It was part of the takeoff of Chinese Buddhism into its greatest period. We have to do it too.

Unless we decide we don't want the tradition; but is there any way (bar zazen) to have now without then? The baby without the bathwater?

Sensei said, I teach you zazen posture, tradition of Dogen. What you do with it afterwards is your affair.

Well, what are we going to do with it?

DOWN TO GODO'S KIT-
chen to prepare coffee, cups and
saucers for tomorrow morning,
note that kitchen floor and table
have been admirably washed,
the latter for the first time in
months if not a year, note third
very large spider trying to crawl out of sink—the first one got
drowned deliberately, the second got removed with a paper napkin
while still half-alive, this one gets a reprieve: if it can figure a way
out before the sink is next filled, good for it.

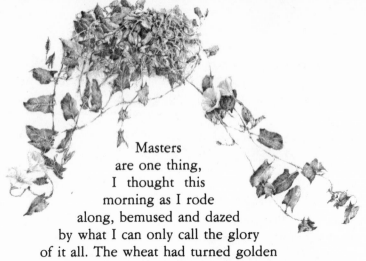

Masters
are one thing,
I thought this
morning as I rode
along, bemused and dazed
by what I can only call the glory
of it all. The wheat had turned golden
almost overnight, the bindweed was blossoming
aggressively, showing itself, in the early-morning light, in every
conceivable degree of closed- and openness, enabling me to add
more and more qualifications, strokes and shades, to my storehouse
of images of it and causing me suddenly to shake my head in
helpless despair because now there is too much to say, too much
shaping and combing of the words, if I wanted to begin to describe
what this one plant looks like, how it grows, how it behaves.

The partridge were there, and one hare and a rabbit, and
orioles and swallows as in other years, confirming my old habit of
belief in permanence, things continuing as they always have; but
more thistles than I remember seeing before (is there such a thing
as a good or bad year for thistles? I'd have thought thistles were
something of a constant in the universe), and more goldfinches too,
which go with the thistles. And also confirming the old habit of
belief was the horse, who is now thirteen and seems hardly any
stiffer or less overwrought and skittish than he did five years ago,
and myself, who am fifty this very day and seem, as far as staring
at cornfields is concerned anyway, exactly the same as I was forty
years ago.

Masters are one thing, thus, as I watched the hops just reaching the tops of the wires they climb on and stared a little unwillingly at the overpowering, heavy midsummer throng of wildflowers crowding one another, heaped and piled and straining silently against the bright, still air, butterflies tumbling everywhere, insects in clouds, the fields sweeping away to the distance striped every green and yellow possible, streams flowing hidden beneath the growth at the bottom of the shallow, broad dips between; but what about disciples?

How does one get to be a disciple?

I could find twenty or thirty biographical incidents, I suppose, that might indicate how this particular one got to be a disciple, but the one that came back to me this morning, the very moment I asked the question, is interesting because it does not concern just my own biography.

Twenty years ago or more I was reading an English periodical one evening at home, the *New Statesman* it was, and it contained a review by someone rather well-known I think, whose reviews I would ordinarily read with respect, of the latest book by the great German philosopher Karl Jaspers. As represented by the critic, what Jaspers had to say, at the close of a long life filled with deep thought, was that however we approached the matter, politically or philosophically, economically or artistically, scientifically or poetically or with bombs, things in general would not get better, the overall human situation would not improve, until each one of us individually got better.

I was just mumbling uncomfortably to myself, Well, that's logical enough, when the critic went on to say that it really was too bad poor Jaspers couldn't find anything more helpful to bequeath us. Is that all? was his contemptuous summary.

I felt a flush of indignation, and shame for those of us who proudly imagine we are educated, for critics and intellectuals, for my own caste. Damned pretentious pen-pusher, who does he think he is, I sputtered.

For whatever else may be the case, it is as plain as day that if every one of us did get better, so would the overall human situation.

That is one way in which a person can become disposed to be a disciple.

DOWN TO LITTLE SITTING room, which is empty and silent. The people cataloguing Sensei's archives emerge from the library behind. Take keys from them, go into library, unlock door to Sensei's room, go to desk, light stick of incense, put in burner on mantel over fireplace, stare at photographs, half-prodded by the memory of the last sight you had of him sitting as close to the fire as he could get, cross and bleak in the April morning, his skin and eyes yellow with jaundice, his gaze miles away, terribly concentrated, and insistent when it met yours, questioning and imposing: tell me if you can, leave me alone if you can't. A sudden pull of himself into focus, giving advice about diet and medical care to a newly surgified cancer patient, giving, giving, brusquely, unmeasuring, giving away all the faith and energy of the universe.

And going away to Japan to die two weeks later, his last gift, leaving us an incomparably rich mess and an absolute drive to carry on with it, however feebly—and we are; and whatever happens— and it has.

The wood sounds outside the dojo.

THERE WAS ONE MOMENT when I was self-conscious and therefore consciously miserable. It was the middle of the night, it was very hot and the women on the window side of the room didn't want the windows open because they minded the draft, there were five of us and all pretty actively sick except one  who was quite old and had been in a mental home for years; she wet her bed and it woke her and she got up and began creeping from bed to bed in the dark in search of a nightgown she could take to replace her wet one, snuffling a little and whimpering and talking to herself in a mildly peeved voice. I had a momentary glimpse of the whole scene with its smells and dampnesses and drips and clicking machines and the batty old woman creeping about, and I did, just that once, say to myself that whenever this is over and whatever the upshot, I am going to some place where there is sun and a warm sea.

The
other even-
ing, still at the
office, I looked out
the window and saw a
blackbird a few yards away on the
edge of the flat roof of the prefabricated
annex in which the language services are housed.
There was something unusual about its bill, it was globulous at
the tip.

In pursuit of some scuttering insect crossing a road, it must
have driven its bill hard into the asphalt, and the asphalt is more
than half-melted in this heat.

So its bill was stuck shut by this blob of tar. I stared at it for
some minutes. It hardly moved, its feathers were unruffled, it
showed no signs of panic; the only thing was, it wouldn't have been
there at all in the ordinary way, but somewhere out of the sun under
leaves or an overhang. It sat and seemed to stare in my direction
but who knows, with birds' eyes as round as they are. Also, now
and then it cocked its head to look skyward where, very high, a few
early swifts were sweeping up and down the lanes. Was it turning
over all the resources of its small brain, trying to imagine a way out
of its dilemma? Did it in any sense know that it was in grave danger?

I thought of ornithologically minded colleagues, but none of
them would have been able to catch it. And the few birds I have
handled myself in attempts to rescue them from cats and other
menaces have, almost without exception, died in my hands, of
fright, I suppose.

I stared on, remembering the famous old Chinese painting with the monk leaning out his window watching mayhem—were they fighting cocks, or a snake and a bird?—and smiling with infinite beatitude and grace, exemplifying detachment. I felt there was a smile on my face, and wondered if it looked anything like his. It felt like a grimace, as of one who has been given a violently unsavory medicine to take and told, "There, now, that wasn't so bad, was it?" But then, maybe that's not what it looked like.

Detachment would come in the end, I supposed, and perhaps after another forty or fifty years of purificatory patience the resentful grimace would be smoothed into innocence. Unless the monk's smile was as misleading as mine.

I looked away, long enough to think this thought, and when I looked back the bird had flown away. Detachment is decidedly easier when there is nothing around to sustain the attachment.

LOCK DOOR, LOCK LI-
brary door, replace keys, greet
godo and bell-girl arriving together, put on kesa, pick up
zagu, papers. The dojo gong re-
sounds clearly through the open
windows. The bonsho-ringer
stands, his robe and kesa hanging heavy in the afternoon heat.
Sandals off, into the dojo, bow, walk around people's backs—fewer
than in the morning because some permanent staff, office and
kitchen, and a few of the video-viewers and their ilk, people for
whom a little "reality" goes a long way, are exempted, or exempt
themselves, from afternoon zazen. Plump up godo's zafu and own
zafu, sit.

Afternoon zazen is a curious time. Some of the nervier people
are tired from working hard in the forest or on the road or roof,
and are at last comfortably relaxed in zazen. Some of the ordinarily
calm just fall asleep, with the buzzing of hornets and the power saw
far away in the woods. The dojo feels less like the center of the
world from which all things radiate than it does in the morning, and
more as though it had withdrawn from what is going on around it.
Children can be heard sometimes, and now and then a metallic
crash in the kitchen, from somebody whose concentration-and-feet
have slipped. There are empty zafus propped against walls and
pillars; one is aware that some people are not there.

THERE WAS ONE HIDEOUS moment in the middle of the flight back to Paris, an air trough that seemed to go on forever, and when the 747 hit the bottom of it everything shook. But that was all. When the plane started down over Paris, Sensei folded his rakusu on his knee, put a hand on it and looked out the window. As the plane touched down he reached his hand over and shook mine, without a word.

One
of these
terribly hot,
flyful mornings I re-
membered a corner of the
woods I seldom visit, except in
early spring to see the blue scilla that grow
wild there. There would certainly be shade and
perhaps cool. We made our way between stiff fields of wheat and
tasseling corn, cantered across a couple of meadows and into the
woods.

Trees really grow very fast, if you aren't there every day to
watch them. Here was a patch we easily saw over the top of a few
years ago, now leaning over us, not defenseless under the sky as
before but becoming secret and private to itself. And shady; soon
nothing will grow at all between the trunks, which is the way they
plan it, the forestry people, but bad for wildlife.

Further along, the path grew quite dark and then boggy. A
drainage ditch crosses it there and the path over the top stays
muddy through the driest of summers. The sudden darkness and
cool and damp, after the brilliance and relentless glare of the morning everywhere else, and the feeling of being in a place the sun
never reaches, that is sodden and squelchy and oozing day in and
day out, brought into my head a word, and I suddenly thought, So
that's what the inside of Hamlet's mind was like! No wonder he
made such a fuss and had such a hard time of it.

The word was "rank." "Things rank and gross in nature possess it merely." I checked the quote later to see if I remembered

it correctly and realized that it was "the world" he was talking about and not the inside of his own head.

But "the world" is, exactly, the inside of one's own head; so I was right too.

I hadn't been sure, also, where the line occurred—in the first act, I thought, but maybe in the scene with Gertrude, and it was her mind or body or behavior he was talking about. I found the quote in the first act but looked at the scene with his mother anyway, and there the word was again.

The brain really is a fascinating affair. I can hardly recall the name of the lesser bindweed, which I took some trouble to learn a year ago. But for *Hamlet,* which I haven't read or seen for a good ten years, the connections, some strong, some tenuous, are still there. I can remember very clearly the evening, something like thirty-eight years ago—I was baby-sitting for some people who lived near the local college—that I spent memorizing "To be or not to be."

One could ask a computer how many times and where the word "rank" occurs in the play, meaning (what does it mean exactly, I think of stagnant water with the wrong kind of algae, the blue-green kind that mantles everything and prevents oxygen from getting to the plants, and a powerful smell that is intimidating, not of normal rot but of some process one might term chemical, as distinct from natural) and not meaning grade or degree, and have the answer in however many zillionths of a second it needs to tell you.

One could, and one would if one had other things to do with one's poetry-making parts.

OUTSIDE THE CLINIC, LIFE
was relatively rosy. There was
the nurse three times a week for
the other injections, and letters
to write to doctors to ask what
they thought about the last results of some test; but mostly
there were friends who came to
visit, only one or two but the
kind who never did anything
particular. I noticed who wrote awkward notes they'd have better
left unwritten and who avoided me altogether, but the negative
things were quickly bypassed and the positive ones stuck. One
woman gave me a miniature rosebush which I have planted in the
garden and it does very well; I have taken that—because I am not
immune to magic, just as I am not immune to skepticism—to mean
that she loves me more than appears to be the case. Whereas another woman gave me a cactus, which I forced myself to try to keep
alive but which was demolished repeatedly by the cat and ultimately
thrown away; and I have taken that to mean that she loves me less
than appears to be the case.

Two or three times, and each time for about five minutes, there
looked like being deep trouble between Jean and me. As I saw it,
the fact that his wife had died of cancer put him in the impossible
position of being unable wholeheartedly to want me to get well.
That may not have been his position at all, in his own mind, but
whatever his position was he kept it to himself. Very luckily, his
reactions when he is pushed are loud and violent, so that I could
see he was pushed and quickly stop whatever I was doing that was
provoking him.

ZAZEN. SIT. KIN HIN. Walk. Zazen. Sit. One hour, hour-and-a-half? Forever? No time? Your knees, if you're a regular sitter for periods of time which are regularly the same, will know how long you've been there to the minute, although even that can change with the weather, amount of running you've been doing or coffee you've been drinking—and I say knees but of course it can be ankles, sciatic nerve, kidneys, shoulders, dorsal muscles or jaw or wherever your particular imbalance happens to be greatest at the moment. But otherwise, there is no measurement of time, time becomes the flexible, subjective nonentity it really is. Time is all existences, says Dogen in a chapter that many people explain quite confidently but I think no one has worked it *all* out yet; and all existences are time. Your conscious mind comes and goes, aware then not aware of posture, breathing, sounds, sensations; blotting out, wheeling to face, recording, drowsing, coming to attention, sometimes poised, briefly in balance, unified, indistinguishable from body and from air-sounds-other-people-tick-of-clock-and-implosion-of-star-in-some-other-galaxy, yet not un-conscious either.

Perhaps
I may unmake
up my mind. The
week has ended so bad-
ly, it hardly sounds plausible;
discretion vis-à-vis the cosmic order may be more appropriate now, and
not this journalistic disclosure of the workings
of its digestive processes.

Attachment. The lessons are falling thick and fast.

Saturday morning the young cat Niblick, of remarkable sweet-
ness of character, did not present himself for breakfast that I prepared and left, assuming he had made one of his occasional trips
along the gutter of our fourth-floor apartment to the neighbor's,
where he is welcome. I went down early to work in the garden:
there were one or two things that absolutely had to be done before
one went away, heat or no heat, taking up the overcrowded iris and
thinning and replanting the rhizomes, and setting out sweet william
for next year. One could only hope that more drenching than usual
and a thick top-dressing of peat might help them over the dangerous days until rain comes. So I hurried to finish before the sun
worked round to the south, and got severely bitten by stinging ants.

By noon the cat was still absent and we began to worry, con-
sulted neighbors, investigated corners of the attic with flashlights,
rang the SPA and ate an uneasy lunch. He could have fallen and
been unhurt and picked up by somebody, or been hurt and hidden
himself—but I was working there all morning, he would have
called—or been killed but then there should have been a cadaver

somewhere. We toured the garbage cans. The newspaper would not take a lost announcement until Monday morning. I ironed clothes and cleaned one fish tank, then at six we decided to go up into the hills anyway for what was left of the weekend, since our presence in town could change nothing one way or the other.

The car turned the corner at the end of the garden and my eyes caught those of the cat, lying quietly under a large bush behind a wrought-iron grill. When I got out of the car he mewed. He was unable to move. Where had he been all day while I was working a few yards away and other people were calling and looking for him in the very place he now lay?

We forced open the grill but couldn't pick him up because of the bush; I drew him protesting between the bars. He had been in heat over ninety degrees Fahrenheit all day but would not drink. We drove to the vet who was on duty that weekend for the whole town. There were several people ahead of us, and each one seemed to take a long time. The cat's head hung down, his breathing was jerky and heaving. When it was our turn the vet stuck pins in the cat's hind legs, said there seemed to be a little reaction as though maybe it wasn't the spine, took an X-ray and showed us the fracture in the tiny frail pelvic bones, and said that if it was his animal he would put it down. There were operations, pins and whatnot, but little chance of success and anyway the animal would never be right, and the cost terrific, and so forth.

It's true he hadn't seemed much of a fighter, not like his predecessors the irascible Siamese dowager duchess and the broad-chested Abyssinian prince; altogether a humbler sort of creature, needing quite a lot of affection and giving quite a lot in return, but nothing excessive. Not so awfully clever and not so striking, but pure of line and sweet of face and gentle in play, with only one trick but a very fetching one, of charging at one, bounding high into the air and turning in midair to land and gallop off in another direction.

I couldn't decide. We left him there to be rehydrated and have further tests done to see whether or not there were internal injuries, thinking we would make up our minds Monday morning when we could consult the regular vet.

We drove off late, after eight, toward the hills. I cannot remember a more beautiful evening in Alsace. I stared at the sweltering fields, blue cabbage, wheat stubble, flowering tobacco, corn still green. Jean put a cassette of the Schubert C Major Quintet into the tape player. I started to cry; there have been several deaths lately among the humans in my world. *Sunt lacrimae rerum.* But it was Mozart, not Schubert, that Stendhal associated with those words, writing about the death of *pauvre Lambert.* There are tears for things.

The silhouette of the Vosges was so exquisite, clear, the lines clean, each gentle range of hills curving blue-gray a lighter shade than the one in front of it. The color, curves, cleanness, soft lines of that poor half-dead cat. We drove on. Over all the other, duller woes lay a thin veneer of excruciation: the burning itch of the bites of stinging ants.

Someone once said, about Sensei's eyes, "Sometimes there is all the sorrow in the world in them." I hadn't seen it. One evening there was a ceremony, and I was directly in front of him as he turned away from the altar. In his stare, pure concentrated intensity, black, depth without end and without meaning, a scorch, a blare of the ultimate nothing he was transmitting to us. I stared back as long as I could.

Maybe that's what that person meant by sorrow.

THE GONG. GET UP, CREAK-
ing and lame, gather papers and
follow godo back to room.
"Change the column-person sitting opposite me," he says; "his
posture's all crooked, it bothers
me. And tell shuso we'll chant
Fukanzazengi tonight."

Shuso is with his wife and children at the other end of camp.
Ascertain with him which of the column-persons has the crooked
posture and who could be asked to replace him and how he could
be asked to move without feeling too mortified; and agree that
shuso will make sure there are copies of *Fukanzazengi* at the entrance to dojo.

Up to own room, eat a cookie and some grapes, staring out at
the copper beech, light a cigarette and sit down to type a translation
of Keizan's precepts for godo to use in ordination ceremony.

"Do not kill . . . the life of Buddha is increasing." What the
devil does that mean? To translate, you have to decide. That the
property of life is to increase? Also, grammatically the Japanese is
apparently more like "No killing" than "Do not kill" and implies
"There is (ultimately) no such thing as killing"; so maybe none of
these should be commands.

"Do not steal. The mind and its object are one." Nice.

"Do not covet"—is that the same as Sensei's "No bad sex,"
which used to worry some of our homosexuals?

THE GREAT THING WAS that because of the extended sick leave from work I could spend most of the summer, except for the weeks of chemotherapy, at La Gendronnière. I had a tiny room to myself and did quite a bit of my own cooking. I had strength enough to go everywhere I had to go and  missed only one zazen the whole summer. The stairs were a long climb but not longer than before. One went slowly, gently, very rhythmically. To a great extent, I learned, energy can be replaced by rhythm. There were days when, driving to Blois to shop or pick people up, I had to use an arm to hoist the leg that shifted gears, but that, again, was what was happening that day.

At one point my blood went all to pieces and the clinic in Strasbourg, to which the results of interim tests made in Blois were telephoned, started ringing me up at the camp and telling me I had to come back and go into a sterilized room. Looking at the couple of hundred people around me who were cheerfully spreading their germs about, I thought, They've got to be crazy to think I'm leaving here to hide in a room where everybody wears gloves and is wrapped in cellophane. I didn't go. The result was that when I duly turned up for my next scheduled week of chemotherapy the clinic had assumed I had interrupted treatment and failed to program me and there was a terrible shouting showdown with the doctor.

Everybody at the camp was, as far as I could see, absolutely ordinary. Nobody did anything special for me and nobody did anything special against me. A girl said something one day about my being a person who had never really accepted being a woman. I gagged on that because it was as much her problem as mine and it felt cruel, in my present de-ovaried, de-uterized circumstances. I complained to Jean who said, The things you are transmitting just now frighten people. I hadn't been aware of transmitting things, but of course I was.

I didn't see how thin I was, maybe I didn't see a lot of things. I was busy.

The
alarm fails
to go off at 6 A.M.
but I wake up by luck
and programming at 6:15,
throw on yesterday's clothes, feed
the ailing cat and give it its medicines
and change the newspapers next to the bathroom sink
where it has been uncontrolledly urinating all night, leaving those
on the floor to be changed later, clatter not too noisily down three
long flights, leap into the car, turn the starter with fierce application
because it is about to give up but really mustn't until the end of next
week when I can let them have it at the garage, drive to the local
dojo in Strasbourg without noticing the kind of day it is going to
be, with at least two of the cross-lights green which is a help and
most unusual, unlock the outer door, unlock the inner door, throw
on robes, wake up the person whose turn it was to sleep there last
night, observe that only one kyosaku-person has turned up, which
is beginning to be a habit although it is true that there are eleven
people at La Gendronnière this week, show the novice kyosaku
how to prepare the incense box, look around when she says the
flowers on the altar are falling apart and find two small vases of
heather to put in their place, sound the wood calling people (What
people? Four in all this morning.) to zazen, hear the gong, the
kyosaku is ready with a stick of incense at the entrance, step in.

Restrain a minor intestinal upheaval until kin hin time, leave
the dojo, remove kesa, do what is necessary, observe that there is
no toilet paper, find some, complete that task while preparing some-

thing scathing to say that night about responsibilities (i.e., upkeep of toilet) undertaken and not carried through, put kesa back on, re-enter dojo.

During the second zazen, read and translate Dogen's seven principles of Zen around which I will be talking the rest of the week. At the end, after the ceremony, change back into yesterday's clothes, make a date for dinner Saturday and try to speak to somebody about a husband who's sick but fail because somebody else is hanging around, drive home, stopping at a pastry shop to buy two rolls, collect the cat, rags, medicines, a cardboard box to hold it all, a book on homeopathic medicine for cats that I want to give the vet, eat one roll standing up in conversation with Jean, down the flights of stairs with cat and box, drive to the vet, sit down and wait while smoking a cigarette and stroking the cat and smiling at a man with a poodle wildly yapping to get at the cat, talk to a woman who says, "A Chartreux, I can't bear to look at it, mine just died and I had it fifteen years," so I explain that it's a Russian Blue not a Chartreux so then she can bear to look at it.

When it's my turn, I discover that the vet is not going to tell me yes or no, only that maybe he will regain bladder control maybe not but we must clear out his system first so in addition to the four products that I am already administering give him these two more and come back in fifteen days (I'll have left by then), oh, all right, make it twelve.

Drive home, empty the cat's car tray in which he has accurately shat and wipe off the seats on which he has helplessly dripped, up the stairs noticing this time that the day is turning fine and pale after a slightly muddled beginning, a high wash of streaky cloud, change the newspapers on the bathroom floor, rub ointment into the patches of mycosis that the poor beast caught while recovering from the pelvis operation at the other vet's, eat the second roll while reading half a column of a criticism of Shakespeare critics in the *Times Literary Supplement,* answer the telephone which never rings at that hour because there's never anybody home to answer it, speak to the woman on the other end of the line in Paris to say that I don't know where the Lycée Couffignac is but since she's arriving from Marrakech via Paris to take up a teaching position there this afternoon why doesn't she come to lunch and we will find out where the school is then, leave a note for Benjamin saying there will be one more for lunch, down the stairs again, pick up the mail, drive to the chemist, order the additional homeopathic medicines for the cat, drive to the office, beg leftover newspapers from the newspaper vendor for use on the bathroom floor, stand in line at the bank checking bank statements received that morning against what I think my balance ought to be, write a check, take the money, drive to the annex, punch the clock (it is almost eleven and we are supposed to be there by nine at the latest), walk into the office and sit down with a blank stare out the window and a grunt.

The placidness of the day outside looks back.

"DO NOT LIE." SENSEI AL-ways said that was particularly tough.

"Do not sell the wine of delusion. There is nothing to be deluded about." That's one that has changed enormously over the centuries; sometimes it's "Don't drink at all," sometimes it's "Don't sell," sometimes "Don't get drunk or make other people drunk," which means that in theory you can't be a wine merchant or bartender, sometimes it's drugs as well as alcohol; which just goes to show the tenacity of human belief that there *is* something to be deluded about.

"Don't criticize others."

"Don't brag or give yourself airs."

"Don't be stingy. There is nothing to be stingy about."

"Do not be angry."

"Do not speak ill of Buddha, *dharma, sangha.*" Dharma is law, or the teaching of Buddha, sangha the community of people who practice.

In every religion's list you find some the same, some different. Sensei said, Once you're ordained you *can't* break the precepts anymore, even if you want to.

It certainly does become more difficult. . . .

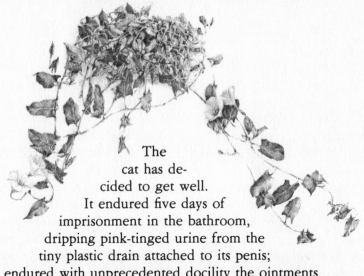

The
cat has de-
cided to get well.
It endured five days of
imprisonment in the bathroom,
dripping pink-tinged urine from the
tiny plastic drain attached to its penis;
it endured with unprecedented docility the ointments
I put on its shaved hindquarters, bedsores and bald patches and the
large and small pills I shoved down its throat, and stoically ate its
way through the medicinal drops sprinkled on its food and the
powders mixed up in it. At moments it seemed to want to play and
began skittering about until its unsteady hindquarters slipped side-
ways and it fell, clunk, with a jarring sound of bone unprotected
by fur, on the kitchen or bathroom tiles. At other moments it
wanted only to be cuddled and stroked and would lie purring,
concentrating on purring. Sometimes it curled into a flat scrawny
pancake of misery with those drops oozing slowly and steadily from
beneath it onto the wads of newspaper we had put everywhere.
Sometimes it was filled with twitches and tremors and quakings;
they were most terrifying because it was not clear whether they
denoted bone pain or digestive discomfort or uric acid poisoning
or what.

Last night when I went to bed it protested from behind the
bathroom door and I went to sleep to the sound of its front claws
shredding newspaper and raking the inside of the door. This morning, when I opened the door, it emerged purposefully and as
though it had a right to be on the outside. I saw at once that the

drain was gone (and, in fact, not to be found—has he swallowed it?) and no drops forming. The newspapers were dry. In the tray, on the other hand, was a small wet patch. He is very pleased with himself, and has taken possession of one of his former favorite places, the middle of the bed. I think that at the level of simple lust what did the trick was his being forcibly separated from his sheepskin rug, the only object (including persons) to which he is deeply —obsessively, in fact—attached. He is not yet entirely out of the woods, but it seems more and more likely that he will make it.

What remains a question in my mind, in regard to those five days, were other moments when he would sit upright, quite far away, not visibly suffering or conscious of anything in his body, not crying for attention or even knowing one was there, but staring intently and thoughtfully at a blank wall, or on one occasion at what I thought might be a fly on the ceiling but was only the ceiling itself. As though some process were coolly debating, through him, but bearing no relationship to his bodily or his psychological state, whether to go on or give up. I would like to know more about that.

SOMEBODY SAID, "THE WEAK egos he gets by intimidation, the strong ones by flattery." Watching him operate, one realized it was true, and learned pretty quickly which kind of ego one had oneself.

There was more than one kind of flattery. There was a kind—"X or Y dojo is best dojo, all others weak"—that made you cross even as it flattered, that was intended partly for people who were not from X or Y dojo so they would feel envious and see their envy and be stimulated but that was like a caution for you too: you're the best today but what will you do to be the best tomorrow? Is it worth it? What does "best" mean?

Childish; one gaped at the childishness of it sometimes; but always, always effective. There was another kind of flattery, occasionally accompanied by an automatically put on, automatically wiped off smile, that was a slap in the face and told you you were in the wrong place at the wrong time. There was another kind, as when he called you back after the morning greeting and said, gesturing at your shaven pate, "Beautiful!," that made you feel very foolish and pleased.

READ THROUGH SHEETS, correct spelling and typing mistakes—not bad stuff this text.

Put on rakusu for evening meal, down to godo again. Shuso stops by to say everything okay for evening, arrange meeting for next day to discuss autumn and winter arrangements for this place, investments, roof repairs, etc. The metal rings from the kitchen, but no godo or bell-girl. Go out on step and look vaguely around. Somebody going past on way to dining room says, "He's at the bar."

Pick up handbell and head for dining room door, collecting panting bell-girl on the way, and arrive at same time as godo, full of plans and ideas, coming from bar in work clothes. Dining room not very noisy tonight, although talking allowed at dinner. Are people tired, is there something wrong, is it just "normal condition" (= *satori,* in Sensei's language)? Or too many potatoes?

Eat, try to listen, cut in and out, stare at bowl of flowers, plates of food, a fork, a piece of paper with a name written on it and a spot of soy sauce in one corner; the grain of boards in the tabletop.

I DON'T KNOW WHAT else to say about how I experienced sickness.

I go to meetings of the cancer group that has started up here in town but don't have time to be more active. What I care about is changing the minds of medical practitioners, changing their training, changing the minds of people who have cancer, opening things up. I am baffled by the evasive tactics of everybody, doctors and patients alike. I don't know what they're being evasive about.

I don't want to be sick and die any more than the next person, but I am so certain that knowing that there are sickness and death —my own sickness and death—is the place to start from.

Start from in the right way. It is not minor and to be smoothed away. It is not a planetary tragedy, it is not a matter of course, and it is not untrue and to be kept hidden.

Sometimes in Europe, sometimes in America even where the whole thing has been opened up so much more but then somehow trivialized again, I think that's where the trouble is, in a wrong or incomplete dealing with "my own sickness and death."

What Buddha did was "solve the problem of life and death." What the Zen masters exhort you to do is, "Here and now, solve the problem of life and death."

"The great matter is the matter of life and death."

That does not mean, "Be serious, don't laugh, assume a solemn air, speak in grave tones"; nor yet, "Have another drink and forget it."

It means, "Find out now, at once, what is the problem of life and death, your own life and death, and solve it."

Yester-
day I was
out early, to
finish riding in time
for Sunday morning zazen
because I was going to have to spend
the whole afternoon in the garden getting
it ready for a month's absence.

There had been heavy rain, the weather was much cooler; the sky was still completely gray, and no wind. I thought it would be one of those place-marking days that come sometimes in summer when nothing happens at all, the season is not going forward or back, somebody has put a cloth over the cage and forgotten to take it off. We headed for the part of the forest where I once saw the five deer but they weren't there; perhaps they had decided the day wasn't happening and they would wait for the next one.

As we went along, quietly through a grave, sober quiet, there was a sudden patch of brightness on a tree trunk off to one side. I looked up; the clouds were thinning and the sun coming through. The patch faded. We rode on. Then more patches of brightness.

Light and shadow. Light and shadow is my delight. I look about avidly, and grin and am dazzled, by light and shadow. Everywhere: underwater diving in the Mediterranean, among the skyscrapers in New York, in one room inside an apartment, here in the forest, flying over countries or oceans.

MU GEN NI BI ZE SHIN I, it says in the *Hannya Shingyo*. . . . In KU (that is, in "reality," "underneath it all"—why is it that philosophical language cannot help but confuse the issue by implying either a place, "in," "underneath," or a time, "originally"?); in KU, or the Void, there are no eyes, ears, nose, tongue, skin, consciousness . . . or anything to be seen, heard, smelled, tasted, touched, aware of. . . . No light and no shadow, that is.

Those are the words Sensei calligraphed on the big sheet that hangs on the wall at home, my own calligraphy with my own name on it . . . that exists no more than eyes, ears, nose, etc. What I particularly need to be reminded of. As always, his excellent intuition, that seemed to happen so much by chance.

Especially in the case of that calligraphy, which he made in Berlin, working very fast on the floor of a room in a Protestant center where he gave his first and only sesshin in that city; one of the local group had brought him a present of some fine paper, so he went to work on it between two zazens in the morning, dashing off huge characters first, one or two to a sheet which I then removed and put somewhere else on the floor to dry while he attacked the next sheet.

Then, when he had done thirty or so, he walked around and pointed to the ones that were to be kept; the rest were destroyed. Then he finished them off, one by one, adding more characters in some cases, in others only his signature. At the end, he or I stamped them with his stamps. Then they were given away or sold, but not for much: that is a Zen tradition. The work of some of the old masters goes for fortunes nowadays, though.

This particular sheet was not the same quality of paper as the ones he did before it; instead of drinking the ink, it left it in pools on the surface. So when I picked it up and whirled to find a place for it and put it down before the next one was ready, the ink all skated to the top of the sheet and flew onto the floor, leaving a series of parallel, diagonal streaks that were not part of the character MU ("not," "in-," "un-") at all. Also, a little later another sheet dripped onto that one, leaving two blots in odd parts of it.

As he was going round the room, he indicated that it was to

be destroyed but his secretary said, "I like it, it's sort of modern art." He considered it again briefly, saw something, and said, "All right, keep." Later, he worked one of the blots into the other characters, which left one. When he asked which calligraphy I wanted I said that one, and he worked the other blot into my name.

Excellent intuition. MU GEN NI BI ZE SHIN I . . . no eyes, ears, nose, tongue, skin, consciousness. No light and shadow.

Fortunately, this is in KU, in absolute reality; and being in KU does not preclude being in the world of light and shadow. Broad-minded people, the Zens.

為南心泰白尼
東仙

色馨香

ANNOUNCEMENTS,
stand up again, more people to
see, about photographs, sale of
posters, someone to meet a
train, photocopies.

Who's this? What's she telling me? Oh: better sit down.
What do you do when there is dissension in a dojo and people don't
know whom to follow?

Punt, I am always tempted to say, but not very many people
this side of the Atlantic would understand me.

That takes quite a while, smoking and leaning over the table
while the cleaning teams clear, sponge and wipe in front of you and
you say the best you can, trying to get the person to show, and then
to see, where she's caught, snagged. And to shove all possible
energy her way so she can go *on.* A funny process, it happens again
and again. . . . You start with a rational exchange and then suddenly
shift gears because a rational exchange is not what is needed; again
and again you waste time rationally exchanging, again and again
you're surprised: to have the energy, to need it, to see that it works.

And walk back half-laughing, to be so stupid, still to be being
surprised, wasting time. Stop and look in the little stream—no fish,
but water lilies. The brown water stares dully back, unmoving.
Where are the frogs that chorus during zazen two or three times
a day?

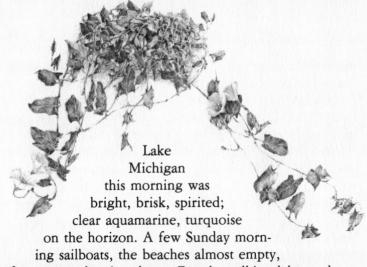

Lake
Michigan
this morning was
bright, brisk, spirited;
clear aquamarine, turquoise
on the horizon. A few Sunday morning sailboats, the beaches almost empty,
two-foot waves slapping down. People walking lakeward
purposeful and equipped, their eyes already seeking and finding the
water as they stood at stoplights on the way. I've never seen the lake
more joyful, grinning.

Later, at a home in the suburbs, there was time to lie flat on
one's back on a terrace and stare up through the heavy canopy of
oak to a sky of unqualified true blue while listening to the loud,
long horn of cicadas; the sound might have been painful except that
it reminded me. I have lived so many years away from it and away
from this thick foliage of oak that I had forgotten. Then, as they
crowded back to consciousness, came a great memory of body, all
of it stretching out, shedding layer after layer of assimilated other
experience, other landscapes and sounds, of defenses perfected and
balanced, until there was nothing left but this, the first. Into this was
I born and in it I rejoice.

And now at night, further in the country, all I hear is the
endless rhythmic sawing of crickets. I half want to say, Forgive me,
I have forsaken you. But only half, because Golden Gate in Alsace
is the life I have chosen and intend. The bedrock, nevertheless, is
Illinois oakleaf and mindless summer insects close around.

The combination of identity recovered, with attendant abate-

ment of the superstructures of life and their pressures, and a multi-
tude of nagging unpleasantnesses and distastes that always awaken
when I am here, is such that there is a strong inclination to inertia,
to do less and less, not move, not think, grow into some small
prettyish clean suburban room and there remain indefinitely, allow
the whole molecule to slow and muddy, petrify. No more in-
security and also no more pain and irritation. Here is womb, here
is "home," here is hearse.

Let nothing happen. Let no one move. Let everyone be as
smooth and devoid of feature, promontory or abyss, light or
shadow, as this past fortnight of portraits of American Olympians
bleating insipidly at the cameras. How one rejoiced to see the
quick, open, nervous smile of the last winner of all, the unexpected,
unobvious thirty-seven-year-old commonplace Portuguese who ran
tired and happy into the arena at the end of the marathon, and in
whom there was nothing more than tired and happy.

One had put up with the American steamroller, one had ad-
mired them, one had from time to time been glad they were "the
best," but there was mounting exasperation too, at the immensity
of this calflike, hormone-sleek collective ego; and real annoyance
at such babyishness as showing only two flags on the screen, two
American flags, when the bronze medal was won by a Chinese.
How can "we" accuse "them" of untruthfulness so earnestly?

What I admire about the Olympians, U.S. or other, the fascination that makes me turn on the television once every four years for
two solid weeks, is the mastery. Every movement is beautiful,
weight lifting as much as fencing, because everything has been
pared away, only the essence, pure gesture, is left. And the contact
—all appearances to the contrary, and they are—with the experience, in every one of those bodies if not in many of the conscious
minds connected to them, of union with the cosmic order, as Sensei
called it. You cannot swim or run or leap that many miles and years
without at least a little every day living.

The place, the bones of the country, are my bones and blood and my sky and soil; but oh heaven, I still now find so often occasion to cringe and snarl for its inhabitants.

IT WAS NEW YEAR'S Day at La Gendronnière and Sensei invited the people who had stayed behind to clean up to have dinner with him. We had all worked hard for days and nights preparing the year-end sesshin and the New Year's Eve party and a very large number of ordinations, and cooking for fourteen people that evening was once-more-unto-the-breach with a vengeance.

Sensei was grumpy because his secretary had been busy cooking all afternoon and evening when he wanted her, and the food wasn't ready to be served until nine or so, when I had to leave. So when everybody else sat down at the table I waited in a corner until it was time for the taxi. My departure was a further annoyance to him.

"You must eat!" he half-roared at me. "I must go," I replied. He liked having everybody around him, and nobody to leave ever, and when they did he was apt to brush them off or make fun of them afterward. And when you did have to leave and he said, "You must eat!" or "You must stay!," your leaving instantly became arbitrary, ill-mannered and not really necessary in your own eyes.

I suppose we all knew that a day would come when we would never leave anymore, but for many of us it was not yet, we had things to do, children to raise, money to earn, or thought we did.

                                        This
                              other place,
                           too: the lake.
                    Just beyond the window
                tonight a constant soft rustle,
             faint night breeze in the dense
        woods around the cottage, oak, birch, red and
      white pine and spruce, poplar, incessantly brushing
leaf against leaf; an owl; raccoons hunting; beaver gnawing trunks
at the water's edge.

There is the temple in the Loire Valley, which is home but has very little to do with "me."

There is Alsace where I spend my life; there is Illinois where I burned in the images, cradled the words for tree, bird, river, house; there is this lake in Wisconsin, the ideal of those words, the level beyond what I can ever see; my mind's eye is here, what I miss most is here. I thought I was at home in any inch of the earth's surface, and so I am; but these last three places also have their homes in me.

Their hooks in me; inclining me to solemnity.

GODO ENTHUSES ABOUT a massage he had before dinner, how cheaply he got his car repaired because he finally figured out the way to the mechanic's heart, the Keizan precept text, and even more Fuke and Rinzai: the temptation to become a wild, rough monk abiding by no rules except those of the theater of human body-minds in extremis; but there is the other side too, smooth, and the beautiful manners Sensei was always trying to teach us, somewhat against his own grain perhaps. Godo goes off to reread the story of the seamless garment, sitting a few minutes at the desk, coming out to exclaim, calling for the head cook to discuss the menu for the party tomorrow night.

The wood sounds outside the dojo. Remove rakusu. Smoke a cigarette. Put on kesa. Pick up papers, zagu, sutra book. Empty ashtray. Stare at surface of table which needs waxing every day and seldom gets it. Bell-girl comes. Gong in dojo. Godo comes out. Crunch across gravel, past bonsho-ringer dim in dying light. Sandals off. Few people in gaetan. Bow. Walk around. His zafu, your zafu. Sit. Three bells and wait for bonsho—maybe he didn't hear the third stroke? Ah, there he goes.

bonsho

"THE WAY IS NOT NEAR or far, not easy or difficult; but one must not choose." A very loose rendering of the first lines of the *Shin Jin Mei,* seventh-century Chinese.

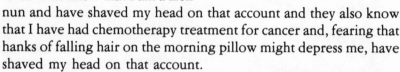

Here's one more thing I can write about sickness:

Most of the people I have to do with know that I am a Zen nun and have shaved my head on that account and they also know that I have had chemotherapy treatment for cancer and, fearing that hanks of falling hair on the morning pillow might depress me, have shaved my head on that account.

At least two of the people I have to do with, and both of them pretty close to me, upon hearing that the old skull was again in evidence this summer, automatically enquired, "Oh, has she been having more chemotherapy?"

Cancer is their choice; but they must not choose. It is not good for me or for them. It is, above all, inaccurate.

It is so hard to see what I mean until you see it. Then it is so easy that it becomes very hard to see what one used to see before. Yet it's all the same mountain.

I DIDN'T LIKE TO ask questions; I was afraid. But one day he was talking about people who had become disciples, this one who had been a fervent Catholic and that one who had found a new faith, and so forth; and I thought, I never had a "faith" at all, what am I doing in this *galère?*

So a couple of weeks later I went to Paris on purpose to ask a question on Sunday morning. I said, "The other day you talked a lot about faith, as though the only people who came here were people who had faith or had lost faith. I don't think I ever had any faith. Is it necessary?"

His interpreter translated into Zenglish. He misheard, or pretended to mishear: "Face?" Wiping around his own face with a hand. "Face?" Laughter. "Oh, faith!" (which he pronounced "face").

He started to talk and talked for minutes and I heard not one word; but I saw, at one point, his hands gesticulating, as though reeling something out of his stomach.

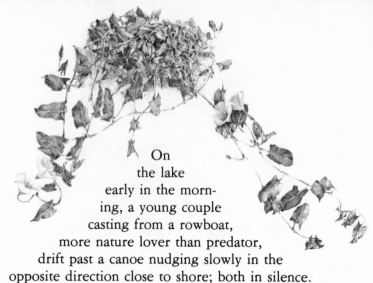

On
the lake
early in the morn-
ing, a young couple
casting from a rowboat,
more nature lover than predator,
drift past a canoe nudging slowly in the
opposite direction close to shore; both in silence.
An osprey patrols overhead, woodpeckers hunt through the trunks,
a flock of chickadees scour. On the surface billions of waterbugs
rush round in circles, their patterns overlying the complicated geometry of underwater reflections flickering against a third complicated pattern of the edges of matted oak leaves, brown and thick,
spread above the ooze. Pattern on pattern on pattern, motionless
leaves under rollicking webs of light under scrolls of insect tracks.

In the shallows on the west side of the lake, where the sun
strikes first rising over the eastern trees, where the ice first melts
in spring and the water warms, lie spawning holes. I've visited them
for forty years but they have had no reason to move for thousands;
and they are made fresh each spring on those days before anybody
has noticed that winter is over. Roughly circular depressions in the
bottom mud or sand or pebbles, the center fanned clean by fins,
leaving a round gravel area a foot or more across where the spawn
is deposited to hatch.

At three or four points around the lake in very shallow water,
a scatter of shell fragments shows where clams can be found in the
ooze. There are usually one or two big ones lying two-thirds
buried. Near them are some large submerged stones, a fringe of

clean bottom around them—can there still be crayfish here, after all these years of motorboats and boys?

Drawing out from there into deeper water, the paddle attracts larger fish, bluegills and sunfish. They hang back watching, two or three at a time, and the sunlight catches a flirt of pale yellow and blue on a fin as they turn and dart.

Small sapphire dragonflies that the French call *demoiselles* streak past, from time to time a huge brown one big as your fist; six or eight swallows skim the surface twittering amicably; and as many least sandpipers, the first I've ever seen, fly past following the shoreline rather timidly, as though they were just passing by and preferred not to be noticed.

The blueberries are on the bushes but mostly still green. Ferns, mosses, sprigs of baby tree, wintergreen, spikes of flag, pine-barren milkwort, goldenrod; a mound of branches on the shoreline the size of a small car means that the beavers have extended their domain since last autumn, when there were seven dams and two big houses in the middle of their pond. Not a twig-snap, not a creak from them in the daytime, though.

Small pocks in front mean frogs hopping in as the canoe edges closer. Almost the same sounds heard at one's back mean the striking of a line cast from the rowboat. The weight of silence, weight of sounds, balanced, shaped and framed by a wide clear pale blue sky.

Lake conversation, boat to boat:

"Looking for anything?"

"Whatever there is."

SILENCE. NIGHT GATHERS and rustles, almost no birds, a thin peep now and then. A hornet trapped in a lampshade. The kyosaku on his rounds clatters down the outside stairs above the dining room. Sound of claws, clicking irregularly on the floor outside the doors—the lame old dog. A heavy thump as he leans against the door to ease his fall, and a sigh as he drops his head onto his paws.

Zazen. Kin hin. Zazen. Godo intones, *"Fukan-zazen-gi-i-i."* Papers rustle: we don't know it by heart. The slow chant begins, accompanied by the wooden fish to keep us together. After a few minutes, pause. The 220 voices in harmony eddy around and around and out into the night, flowing like layered currents in the ocean.

Nothing mysterious in the text, only Dogen's instructions, highly specific and practical, for zazen, seven hundred years old. Like ocean currents, shallow and deep, turning and flowing.

It takes us at least twenty minutes. The silence at the end is thunderous.

"Kai-jo." The drum sounds the hour again, the wood on the gaetan rolls three rolls, shuso strikes the bell once. Godo is already on his feet and bowing "Good night" and he's gone. The time to pick up the paraphernalia, there's a dense throng all trying to get out at once without actually assaulting anybody. The night lights on the bonsho platform throw faces and figures in the dark into theatrical poses; people always cluster there after evening zazen, talking and smoking before they move off to bed, bar, bathroom or other destination.

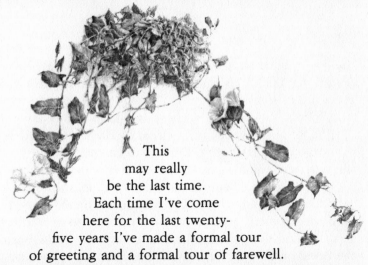

This
may really
be the last time.
Each time I've come
here for the last twenty-
five years I've made a formal tour
of greeting and a formal tour of farewell.
I've gathered leaves and needles from all the trees
to press and carted them from country to country straining the
covers and staining the pages of high school yearbooks until they
crumbled. I've taken pictures of bullfrogs on logs, does drinking at
dawn, pickerel weed spiking against the sky, water lily stems spiral-
ing out of the muck, and stuck them in mirrors on vanity tables,
tucked them into flaps of stationery folders, slipped them behind
tickets in passport holders. Lest I forget.

As though they could help me to remember. I never photo-
graphed the loon or the scarlet tanager, the kingfisher or the ruby-
throat; or needed to. I am not likely to forget how they looked,
flew, what was behind and in front of them, or the time of day or
year. Yet a photograph can do something. Can it show you the reek
of resin radiating from the savagely torn trunk of a great pine
tumbled into the water, slender strips of wood still holding across
the wound like threads of flesh? If you were there and smelled, it
can. And, if you were there, a photograph of the whole lake white
under the high summer sun with its heavy fringe of trees almost
black around it can bring halfway to consciousness the sound, the
never-ending whisper and rustle of leaf. The voice of the lake.

Wherever I am on earth it is enough to lie flat on my back on the ground and stare up at the sky, to know from the sound or silence that that other place is not this one and to partly remember the voice of the lake.

Why remember? Why this business of lest-we-forget?

I have heard that culture is what's left when you have forgotten everything you learned. Culture is to be transmitted. If you can't transmit you haven't existed. Is that it?

So what of a favorite Zen story, of the old hermit in the mountain who said, when asked why he was up there and how long he'd been there, "A long time ago there were two bulls fighting by the seashore; they fought and fought and finally disappeared into the ocean, and from that day to this I cannot remember a single thing."

It is necessary to remember and transmit that story about forgetting, about getting beyond dualism, right-left, fighting bulls.

We must know not-two, non-duality as they say in books; but all we can (and must) transmit is two, the ten thousand things, you and me and the smell of the pine tree.

That's not the whole story, of course, but unless you meet a master in one form or another it will be.

Live every day is not one or the other, not either, not neither, not both. Don't get me wrong.

CRUNCH ACROSS TO Godo; through the door panes a good twenty people can be seen inside—what's up? "Bring everything there is to drink—Heidi and Bernard are leaving tomorrow." Grab somebody and a couple of wastepaper baskets and clatter down to cellar, collect beers, couple of bottles of white wine and fruit juice. Up again, send for glasses and start opening and pouring. Much conviviality and teasing and some reminiscences of days when godo and Bernard were living together and how Bernard met Sensei. ". . . And I fell into his eyes, you know, and that was that."

One certainly did fall into his eyes, but he wasn't at the bottom of them.

ONE HORRIBLE TIME IN Switzerland, I sat and wept and
wheezed and swore and strained and raged, hour after hour for
three days, and toward the end, Sensei's voice coming from a long
way away through the bone-ache and weariness and out of a long
silence, "I'm tired now, too. Pain is not such a bad thing. Pain can
be good." And I hated the voice, said to myself, Goddammit, it
is masochism, fascism, no matter what he says! There *is* something
sick about all this! And afterward, walking past him on my way out,
I glared stonily to express my anger, but it was not noticed: he was
talking quietly to other people. I drove home through the night
very fast and hard and angrily, went to bed and got up the next
morning and went to work and came home and said, at dinner that
night, "I'm going to ask to be ordained."

"Good God, do you know what you're doing!" somebody
said.

(No; really not, not in the slightest.)

"Of course she does," said somebody else.

I laughed.

Beethoven's
Triple Concerto,
broadcast from Meno-
monie. A powerfully redeem-
ing feature in this land
of plethora: that a nowhere like
Menomonie (But *which* Menomonie? Talk about
plethora! When I want to honor the nowhere by spelling it correctly, *Webster's Geographical* says, Menom*inee* pop.
10,099; Menom*onee* Falls pop. 27,845; Menom*onie* pop. 12,769, all
in Wisconsin. Help! That's what I get for calling them a nowhere.
How the hell do they tell themselves apart?) should have a public
transmitter that sends out classical music, good bad and indifferent
pretty much indiscriminately, nonstop.

The table has been cleared.

Night is drawing in on the lake. The wind has dropped almost
entirely, the water becomes a flat silver-gray mirror, the trees'
multiple greens fade to uniformity. Water skiing has packed up for
the day, the cocktailing pontoon boats have chugged home; there
may still be a cousin out there fishing somewhere.

I sit staring through the branches out to the lake below and
across to the far shore, where I can just make out two slim pale
poplar or birch trunks leaning toward the water side by side, exactly
parallel.

There is a sorrow; is it the only one we ever know, the sorrow
of mortality, impermanence?

This lake has been passionately loved by five generations of us
—so few, but in this country, enough. Change has been resisted, by

cunning, regulation, goodwill, bullying, and ultimately money; but some or all of these commodities are now lacking. One might be tempted, from the endless cyclical, boring and bickering rehearsals of the situation that eddy round, to blame it on "socioeconomic" factors, the dispersal of successive generations and their fecundity combined with falling bank balances. Not so, enormously not so.

The American ego that made the place possible, when multiplied by thirty or forty, means a full-fledged feud. Everybody loves it enough to want it all for himself or herself, and the better trained love it enough to be prepared to share it with their own ilk as long as their particular fragment of it remains inviolate, but I think nobody loves it enough to subordinate the individual interest to the general one. Also, these people are beset by the problem of planners the world over, in their conceit: who can imagine what will be the general interest once our own egos are no longer living to define it? Who knows what our grandchildren will want? And the fact that, if history can tell us anything at all that is true, they will want what we want now, is not weighty enough. And we have drifted so far from ourselves that we can no longer imagine at all what the lake wants.

The murk and muddle of human dealings is saddening; but it is not wholly that, that brings this sense of sorrow tonight. It is also the simple drawing in of night, falling of the wind, fading of the silver mirror and its green frame; breathing with the earth's twilight breath.

Against the fading and the falling, we have told tales. If there be night without, let us draw together around the fire or lamp, and devise.

As:

When the cottage was built, the workmen had to come out early in the morning and stay all day, the lake is so far from anywhere. So they brought their lunch. The last ones in the place before the family came to take possession of it that summer were the carpenters and cabinetmakers. Every inch of the inside of the cottage is lined with wood, even under the staircase. And all the kitchen cabinets are wood too, including corner ones with whirly-dos inside that you can spin round in search of garlic salt but find only six jars of mustard. They were a pleasant trio, the cabinetmakers, and took a leisurely meal downstairs, safe from the elements since all roofs and windows were finished before they started. And when they left, they bequeathed to the family a deer mouse that had kept them company and eaten their crumbs.

Or it bequeathed itself.

The first few days it was not in evidence: there was a grandmother, her daughter, her son and daughter-in-law and their three children, a dog, and numerous guests. The party was continuous, everybody had to come and inspect the new cottage and praise and be envious or contemptuous. The place was full of noise and settling-in.

After a few days the parents, dog and third child went away, however, leaving the grandmother, daughter and two grandson-nephews, aged eight and ten. The boys slept downstairs and fairly early, the aunt and grandmother upstairs and they were quiet types, so pretty soon the mouse appeared, having quickly discovered where the kitchen was and that there were things in it of interest.

The grandmother, as is often the case, was sensitive to mice and a light sleeper. She got the first glimpse, and announced the next morning, in a highly accusatory voice, that there was a mouse in the house. Her daughter was fond of animals and said it wouldn't eat much. The boys just wanted to see it.

That evening they were working a jigsaw puzzle on the far side of the room and they did see it, scurrying across the dining area toward the kitchen and disappearing under the refrigerator.

At breakfast the next day they discussed the mouse, and their grandmother set her jaw and went to town to do the shopping. She returned with a good old-fashioned mousetrap, which she baited with excellent Wisconsin cheese and placed along the path the boys had told her it had taken the night before. The boys were not very happy about the trap, their aunt even less, but they bided their peace.

The next morning the trap was empty and unsprung. Aunt and boys crowed with delight, clever mouse. Grandmother was quite cross and not far from suspecting that somebody who was not a mouse had removed the cheese. Her unspoken idea helped to harden the opposition; there was a definite split from then on between the oldest generation and the other two, who seized upon this pretext to become friendlier than they had been before.

That evening the trap was again baited and set, and grandmother and boys went to bed in some degree of tension and anticipation while the aunt, who had proposed to stay up late and observe, laid out a piece of work on the dining room table. It involved gluing pheasant feathers, which came from a cock-pheasant presented and eaten in Scotland, onto the front of a waistcoat. It was a job requiring absolute concentration and no breath of air. The aunt worked away for a while, standing back from the table to inhale and bending over it to pick up the feathers and place them one by one as she slowly exhaled. She heard the mouse as soon as it began stirring, and stood back to watch it. It came quite fearlessly along, to within a mouse-pace or two of the trap, stopped, considered, moved to one side, reached out and deftly extracted the cheese from the trap, considered again, then hurried away to eat it somewhere else, or store it. The aunt laughed, blowing a few feathers onto the floor.

The next morning at breakfast she told what she had seen, and the grandmother expressed great disgust: she was pretty sure that the combined energies of the other members of the family were responsible for the prowess of the deer mouse. She was disgusted, but also aware of being in a minority.

That day she unburdened herself to the caretaker's wife who

lives in a cottage a few hundred yards away, and this worthy told her that what was needed was a Have-A-Heart trap, which would catch the animal but not kill it. It even appeared that she possessed such a thing.

The grandmother, a good loser but also determined to be rid of the mouse, informed her gloating daughter and grandsons about the Have-A-Heart trap. The daughter was a little disgruntled, being the type to favor mice in the house, but was also curious, and the two boys were extremely eager to see how it worked.

The trap was duly procured and proved to be rather rusty and bent but possibly serviceable. It was a wire cage with a trapdoor that fell when the bait was touched and to the pro-mouse faction it did not look any more daunting, for a mouse as clever as theirs, than the other trap. It was baited and another expectant night ensued. In the morning the trap was empty and the cheese was gone; but the door had fallen shut. The mouse had escaped through a loose place in the wire. The boys tied and taped and twisted and made the trap proof against anything less than wire-cutters. That night the aunt slept on the sofa in the living room so as to witness events and possibly intervene. She had drifted off but was not sleeping soundly and heard the sharp, definitive clank of the trapdoor falling shut. She turned on a light and saw that the mouse was well and truly caught, and trying hard to find a way out. It soon gave up, however, and crouched there waiting for something to happen. The aunt went back to sleep.

At dawn she woke, saw that the mouse was still there and fretting again, and went downstairs to wake the two boys. Five minutes later the three of them assembled by the pier, shivering slightly in the chill. They turned the canoe right side up and slipped it into the water, the older boy got in front to paddle bow, the younger one sat in the middle with the trap and mouse, and the aunt paddled stern. They set off across the lake.

A mist or light fog lay on the water and they could not see the other shore. There was not a breath stirring, no sound but the water dripping from their paddles. Suddenly, when they were nearing the middle of the lake, the mist began to run. It ran away very quickly, to the north. They stopped paddling: it was magic. In the most complete silence, there was the mist rushing past them and away, leaving behind it the dawn of a hot summer day.

They paddled on, bemused. When they got to the other side, they beached the canoe and got out, carrying the cage. They had a sense, as they left the water and entered the forest, that it was late, that all the night creatures were hidden, underground in the myriad holes in the infinitely soft ground, the deep humus deposited by centuries of pine needles and fern and moss and mushrooms and blueberries, or between the roots of trees. That the day predators were already awake.

It was late, but it was the best they could do. They chose a large tree that looked as though it had many hiding places among its roots, opened the trap and the mouse ran out. It was dazed and frantic and on unknown ground. It shot somewhere out of sight.

They turned back and paddled across the lake to breakfast with grandmother.

The balance among all four of them had shifted, slightly, subtly, because of the mouse, and years and years later the story was told, to new wives by the boys when they grew up and to old ladies at bridge tables by the grandmother and to friends in foreign lands by the daughter.

What keeps it alive for them all, for their relationships have changed and changed again a million times since then and a million things weightier than a deer mouse have happened to them all, is that no one will ever know whether the mouse made it or not, and that leak is the lifeline.

PEOPLE SAY, WHAT IS the attraction? The man doesn't sound at all lovable; how did you er, um? (They are tempted to say "get hooked"; but since one does not otherwise come on like an impressionable innocent they look for a more suitable term, and don't find it.)

On the dedication page I call Sensei "great bodhisattva of modern times." A bodhisattva is somebody who lives in the world, shares and suffers everything that goes on in the world, in order that other people can begin to find their way. A bodhisattva does not count or measure or keep score. Socially, he may be involved in transactions. Physiologically, he may be drunk. Psychologically, he may be trying to please his dead father. He looks like anybody else; but if he practices, underneath he is not the same.

Sensei is dead; never mind about his personality. All the big booming words one could use about him are really not going to answer the questions of people.

So I shall say no more about his lovableness or otherwiseness than is indicated elsewhere in these pages.

I can say this: the quiddities of a master are not what make a master. I never even noticed a great many of Sensei's quiddities. What I noticed was that I felt total trust and confidence, for the first time in my life. In the experience of total trust and confidence, nothing resists. In the experience of nothing resisting, is harmony and freedom.

What inspires total trust and confidence is, inter alia, the fact that the master does not want anything from his disciple. There is no possibility of abuse. A master may scold and rant and lash out, may resort to trickery and knavery in teaching your tricky and knavish ego, but a master is not trying to seduce you or possess you or do anything to you. Except, when you start pecking at the shell, help you out of it.

JESTS FLY, SOME SHARP, some silly; some go home to a target, some bounce off, some are drowned in roars of laughter.

When people start looking around for more to drink and there isn't any, conversation falters. Godo resolves the situation by leaping to his feet and sweeping everybody off to the bar. Collect glasses, take up and wash, empty ashtrays and clean tabletop, take empties down to cellar, hesitate, head for bar.

Pause in front of crêpe stand where there's a line, and decide not to have one. Pause with lascivious eye in front of the cakes and pies, sneak fingers forward while chatting and capture a few crumbs, ease down to bar and order a beer, look around, head for a friend and sit, observe. After a while, move out to the bonfire that burns every night, sit on a tree stump and stare at the fire and the faces, mournful, mischievous, sulky, pensive. Exchange words, a hug, here and there; sit for a few minutes next to a girl whom you've just begun to know, over a conversation about abortion and men and women.

Men and women. Here in the sangha the relations between the sexes are an exact replica of the rest of society, but also different: however much we carry our karmas with us and are enacted by them—here at the bar, for example—we know that they are not the whole story, not absolute. So although girls may cling and flirt and occasionally get beaten nobody ties them down to any final definition of themselves; they and everybody else know they can change, can be free, are free; and although the men can be macho and boring it is clear that they respect the women too, sometimes in spite of themselves. There are betrayals, upheavals, incidents; as Sensei said, "Phenomena arise." And vanish away very quickly.

And tomorrow morning the men and women will all be on their zafus again, sitting as straight as they can and grappling as best they can with their hangovers and cowardices and delusions of goodness or wickedness.

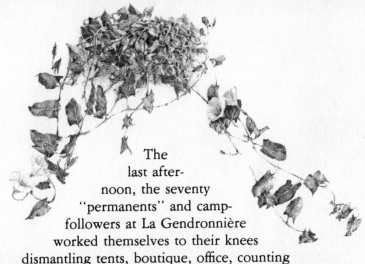

The
last after-
noon, the seventy
"permanents" and camp-
followers at La Gendronnière
worked themselves to their knees
dismantling tents, boutique, office, counting
brooms and tins of Ajax, laying naïve and wicked
plans for next month in Canada and next week in Majorca, while
an end-of-the-world wind from the ocean brawled and slammed in
the trees, seasons revolved, the artificial pond was artificially emp-
tied and appalled desolation swept over the place.

The last-night party had hardly begun shortly after 1 A.M.
when I left it, dancing and drinking itself to stupidity and/or brutal-
ity and/or exaltation, to splash my way back to my room through
the howl and roar of the Atlantic storm-tail.

Tomorrow, Monday. After two months of Real Life, everybody has to go back to Real Life.

THE LIGHTS-OUT CLAP-
pers suddenly arrive, out of the
dark with their blocks of wood,
pacing slowly and clapping in
alternation, slow-quick-quick,
slow-quick-quick, one then the
other; they pass through the bar
and on, separating.

Leave the bar to wear itself out, walk back in pitch dark, feet
stumbling over bumps in the ground, wet grass, a puddle, other
silhouettes moving in various directions, the clappers sounding,
one ahead, the other off to the left, one note a little higher, the
other a little more insistent; impossible to eliminate personality,
however standardized a gesture becomes. Personality of two blocks
of wood and two other blocks of wood from the same tree; of two
people striking them together. The whole wealth of Oriental un-
derstanding, aesthetics—total freedom, unconscious, in rigidly pre-
scribed forms. Provided, of course, one is not asleep.

the clappers

WHEN YOU WERE WELL and truly wrapped up in layer after layer of ego and hours and hours of zazen had brought them all to the outside, you were a dense huddle of discontent and aching joints, morose, standing glumly outside a toilet door somewhere, a pure and perfect image of a three-year-old child caked with resentment, having been ground to a halt by the sheer weight of yourself, nowhere to go, nothing to do, the middle of the night, no thoughts in your mind, and not for the first or maybe even the tenth time but for the last, he would happen along on his hurried way from somewhere to somewhere and give you a big grin and thunder, *"Ça va,* Monsieur or Madame Soandso?" And it would all fall away and you would say, *"Ça va,* Sensei."

That was his intuition. To us it seemed magical, because we had none at all or close to it. It wasn't always operating, though, and he himself admitted that unless he was really concentrated he couldn't know for certain when people were lying to him.

They often did. It was a heroic undertaking for a Japanese steeped in discipline and carefulness, however liberated from them he may have become by his practice, to find himself at the head of a gang of clumsy and unruly adolescents of every age in the guise of disciples, having to be scoutmaster and parent and zookeeper to all these people who were forever trying to trip him up and forever

relying on him for everything. And he had to keep his nose clean, too, and act in such a way that the rabidly protectionist French could not lump him in with all the "sects" around threatening their children's Cartesian pseudo-independence; and hope that we would act in such a way too.

We often didn't. We had our share of noisy nuts, we had a spectacular suicide, we had a few who fell by the way and became true Zen bums begging drinks and mouthing wisdom. We had no inkling of the weight we were upon him, the danger; no inkling of what he had invested in us and had to be ready literally at every instant to abandon—for detachment was the price of success.

What we saw was someone asking a question, "What does a Zen master *do*?," heavy with political and psychological innuendo, and him answering, "Very easy, to be a Zen master. In the morning I wake up, secretary bring tea and shaving things except when she sleep too late, I shave face, clean tooth, put kolomo, come to dojo for zazen."

Spring
was a murky
affair, summer is
said not to have come
at all but I was away for
a good bit of it and can't say, and
September was an all-time low, solid rain
and cold. The grapes that started out the summer
so bravely are still green, except where they've rotted on the vine
(I was condoling with a peasant the other day over the failed crop
and what a shame it was there would be no wine this year, but he
was an honest peasant and said, "Oh, with sugar we'll manage"),
people's gardens in the villages are full of green tomatoes, one
mistakes blackberries for raspberries at a distance because the
blackberries haven't ripened either, and all in all one was about
ready to give up on Alsace.

But then October. I've known this weather several times over
the years. Fog every morning, lifting at eleven or noon or sometimes not until two in the afternoon, then warmth and a pale sky
and sun all benign; real tear-jerking weather.

The other morning I was riding through the mist, tiny drops
were condensing on my face, the tall weeds on either side were
festooned and draped in gossamer, what a wonderful word; but not
gossamer glinting as the sun strikes it and dazzling one with its
geometry, and not gossamer sparkling and beaded with dew, making diamonds or pearls according as the light that catches it is clear
or muffled: this was clotted gossamer, cottage-cheese gossamer, so
heavy with water that it had turned like a bad mayonnaise.

But farther away, the meadows, and beyond them the line of the forest edge, all their bright colors dulled to a uniform bluish green or bluish tan by the moisture in the air. Yet they could be seen to be glowing, brilliantly even, one could see that the sun was shining brightly upon them despite the mist; but it was as though the light was coming from the grasses and trees themselves and not from some source outside. The whole world was glowing, all by itself.

Then in the afternoons, instead of moisture there is something like dust but much finer, some almost invisible particles through which the mid-October sun slants and spreads and pinkens everything, the farmers working overtime to get the crops up and the earth plowed and the seed in, and every field aroar with tractors and combines and men and women knocking over cabbages and topping beets. The plums have somehow ripened and the ground beneath them is black with fallen fruit—few get picked anymore, I suppose it doesn't pay—but the apples that were so promising are paltry and the pears, though there are thousands on the trees, wet and tasteless and quickly rotting, many before they fall. Only one hen pheasant this whole afternoon, so the shooters must have been out on days when I wasn't and swept the place bare.

That pink that isn't pink at all, and the terrible light, gay sorrow, and the bright moodiness in the air: I was first brought to my knees by them in the city of New York on football afternoons; then in Venice, where one hardly dared to breathe, it was so languid and pale and chuckling softly; and then in Paris that day, when I had gone in the morning to see an older woman, one of my real mentors, who was dying and did not quite know it, sitting in bed and eating applesauce and talking about translations and how one did best not to look at one's own once they were published because one could never, never finish fixing them.

I left, feeling heavy and angry, and went to lunch at Lasserre with the first publisher I ever worked for, and the lunch was so good and we got along so well and the afternoon was so much like today—time had slowed, expanded, there was all time in every direction, and every person in the streets was dilated, enshrouded in large thin balloons of musing nostalgia—that we started to walk back from the restaurant, along the Boulevard Saint-Germain; but we had also had quite a lot to drink so that when we came to a furniture shop with some good antiques in its window and an excellent modern copy of a large, low Louis XV canapé, all its cushions filled with real down and covered in reddish-brown velvet, we were through the door and sprawled on the velvet in a flash and twenty minutes later I had ordered one and paid for it—a lot of money, perhaps more than I would have paid if I hadn't been angry and heavy and sad too—and were back in the street again.

So that the balance of these October afternoons, their perfect balance and spaciousness, is almost more than one can bear.

Then this afternoon as I was riding back to the stable, I saw a small bent figure standing under a chestnut tree next to the paddock, staring at the ground. I wondered if it could be he. I have seen him four or five times a year over the last eight years, almost always on his bicycle and always alone, a little old man, meager, his face almost unnaturally triangular, wide at the top and tapering sharply along the cheeks to a tiny, firm chin. His eyes are bright and every time I pass, on the horse or in the car, alone or in company, I wave and smile and he smiles and waves, a wonderful narrow V of a grin full of mischief and delight. We had never spoken. Today I rode over to make sure it was he, and it was; and I saw that he was growing very old and bent at the knees.

I asked if he was finding anything. He took his time, and I thought maybe he was one of the few who really don't understand French at all, but then he opened his hand and in it there were three chestnuts. I said, "Not much, is it? The children have probably picked them all up."

And he answered, "There's enough."

A HUGE SKYFUL OF STARS, sharp and definite here where there is no city skyline to wash the night out.

Through the main door, through the entrance hall that is gaunt and forlorn at night or any time when it's not full of people—correction, at any time full stop; but leaning toward the positively inhospitable at night. Up two tall flights—how many vertical miles does one travel in a day here?—to room. Remove collection from kimono sleeve, throw away used Kleenex and obsolete notes, make new notes for tomorrow, prepare pants, wool T-shirt, kesa. Stand wondering how many layers to take off before going to wash—depends on how cold the air. Take them all off, it's simpler, put on nightgown—needs washing—take towel, soap, toothbrush and paste down hall to bathroom behind sewing-room—windows wide open, at least nobody's left the iron on tonight. Wash, back to room, deposit things. Twenty drops from one bottle, teaspoonful from another. Set alarm. Stand surveying. Pull bed open, collect ashtray, cigarettes and lighter, turn out ceiling light, place sandals, climb into bed, pull sheets, stare around; pick up deck of cards, shuffle and deal four hands, arrange, bid and play two hands of bridge and a game of Canfield solitaire.

Get out of bed, open window, quickly into bed again and turn out light before the insects get you. Sheets cold, don't stretch out yet. The film becomes very sharp for a moment, then begins to fade and jerk. The owl hooting. Footsteps crunch across the gravel below—who? The sheets settle closer.

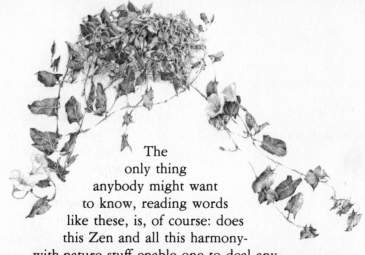

The
only thing
anybody might want
to know, reading words
like these, is, of course: does
this Zen and all this harmony-
with-nature stuff enable one to deal any
better with those times when long, close and enforced
contact with a person, persons or situations bruises every sensibility,
flays every nerve ending, assaults the intelligence, bores the mind
to blindness, thwarts the heart and imprisons the body?

Yes.

Question and answer are both senseless but, having embarked upon this exercise in words, I may as well say it: yes.

But that is really not the point; not the whole point, anyway. The sharp end of the point is that there is no point.

You bring your uneasy ego to a doctor, or a priest or a shrink or a dojo, or a garden or a horse, because you want to get better or freer or richer or more womanly or virile or more peaceful or whatever, and in every case, to my knowledge, except that of a dojo with a good master in it, you may get what you wanted but all that does ordinarily is make room for something else for you to want. In the case of the dojo what you get, for wanting, is nothing.

(That is why, with the exception of gen mai, I have not found any proper recipes to put in this book and, having more or less promised them, I apologize.)

That is the great difference, the great game, the only human adventure, the great freedom. But it is so dangerous that it should probably never be said outside a dojo. It does not imply negativity. It does not imply that anything goes. You have to find out what it implies.

Which reminds me of the other American campus song (slightly amended) that is so close:

> Be kind to your fine feathered friends,
> For the duck may be somebody's mother.
> Be kind to your friends in the swamp
> Where it's always cool and damp.
>
> You may think that this is the end

A NOTE ABOUT THE AUTHOR

NAN SHIN (NANCY AMPHOUX) was born in Rockford, Illinois, and received her B.A. from Vassar College and an M.F.A. from Carnegie Institute of Technology. Since 1960 she has lived in Europe, primarily in London and in Strasbourg. She has worked as a teacher, theater producer and translator for the Council of Europe. She is the translator of many books, stories and essays from the French, including works by Henri Troyat, Claude Manceron, Edmonde Charles-Roux, Françoise Sagan and Michel Tournier. She is also the translator/editor of several volumes in English by Taisen Deshimaru.